Penny Banks

Around the World

With Values

Don Duer

Schiffer Publishing Ltd

77 Lower Valley Road, Atglen, PA 19310

Acknowledgements

The generosity of a number of dedicated collectors who gave me access to their collections made this book possible. Steve and Marilyn Steckbeck sent a complete photographic library depicting their superb mechanical bank collection. Wonderful days were spent with Harold and Rona Blau, Brian Cleary, Ralph Dye Jr., Larry and Jeanie Egelhoff, Joe Eichler and Gerald Lange and Tamara Watkins to study, photograph, measure and discuss the banks in their collections. Our friends Tom and Loretta Stoddard arranged to have pictures made of a variety of their banks. Dick Soukup, Tom Kellogg, Margaret Majua, David Weingarten and Carl White provided banks and photographs. Thomas Lautz, at the Kreissparkasse Koln (Museum of the History of Money) in Cologne, Germany, sent photographs of some of the unusual European banks in their collection.

Proof reading was provided by Harold Blau, Barbara Francis and Carl White. Mechanical bank captions were reviewed by Sy Schreckinger, and Mike Henry assisted in lead bank identifications. Professional photos and prints were produced by Colonial Photo and Hobby, Steadman Studios, and Wiley & Flynn Photographers of Orlando, Florida. All along the way, encouragement from the members of the Still Bank Collectors Club of America and the Mechanical Bank Collectors of America was sincerely appreciated.

A special message of gratitude is extended to my wife, Christine, for her patience and understanding while I wrote and took photographs forever. And I deeply thank my son, Michael, who helped with all the computer glitches.

Library of Congress Cagaloging-in-Publication Data

Duer, Don.
    Penny banks around the world/Don Duer.
       p. cm.
    Includes bibliographical references and index.
    ISBN 0-7643-0019-9
    1. Coin banks--Collectors and collecting--Catalogs.
I. Title.
NK4698.D83 1996
688.7'2--dc20   96-33470
                             CIP

Printed in Hong Kong
ISBN: 0-7643-0019-9

Published by Schiffer Publishing, Ltd.
77 Lower Valley Road
Atglen, PA 19310
Phone: (610) 593-1777
Fax: (610) 593-2002

Please write for a free catalog.
This book may be purchased from the publisher.
Please include $2.95 for shipping.
Try your bookstore first.

We are interested in hearing from authors with book ideas on related subjects.

A Note from the Author

After the publication of my book *A Penny Saved, Still and Mechanical Banks* (1993), which is a history of American penny banks from 1711 to 1993, my publisher encouraged me to continue my study of the subject with a companion volume to present and interpret a large number of banks from collections around the world. The task was challenging, fascinating and arduous; the result is this compendium of over 1,600 penny banks.

It is difficult to describe a typical penny bank collector. Some are intrigued with history in miniature that fits on several shelves in the study, while others admire the beautiful detailed castings or the colorful lithography on tin. Mechanical bank collectors are excited by the action the bank exhibits. Many see a great investment potential in collecting toy banks. For whatever reason they justify their passion, we do know they are a colorful lot, always seeking a treasure in a mildly competitive way. They comb antique shows and flea markets with a veracity that is hard to match.

It was at one of those antique shows that I first met bank collector Harvey Woollens. He invited me to his log cabin home to look at 500 penny banks that were neatly arranged on glass shelves in his study. Before the evening was over, I had made a new friend and started my adventure into the penny bank collecting world. Harvey would trade me a building bank, because in my professional life I am an architect, for every safe bank I found for him. With my interest peaked, we would roam the country in his pickup truck seeking new treasures for our collections. One of our trips was to Ed Mosler's bank sale, held on the sixth floor of New York's Statler Hotel. Although we arrived 24 hours early, the queue had already formed. A rumor surfaced that Sy Schreckinger paid a proxy to stand in line for seven days and nights, to assure the purchase of Ed's rare *Bread Winners* mechanical bank. Our passion for collecting surely gets the best of our senses.

A few collectors enthusiastically search for banks of a particular type. In just four years, Larry Egelhoff has amassed an extraordinary collection of 1,500 safe banks. He spends a great deal of time with his wife, Jeanie, searching remote shops and closet collections for a rare find. All leads are followed, no stone is left un-turned in his quest for a new specimen. When safe banks elude him, Larry purchases small, hand-stenciled personal safes. Several are perched on ornamental stands in his library. Larry says, "Jeanie and I spend a lot of our spare time in the van searching for new safe banks. You never know where one of those little devils will show up."

With great anticipation, the author recently packed the car and set out on his yearly trek to the national penny bank convention, which was held in Livonia, Michigan, a thousand miles from home. The convention was special because it was the silver anniversary meeting of the Still Bank Collectors Club of America (SBCCA), a group whose purpose is to stimulate knowledge and interest in collecting all types of still banks. Generally speaking, still banks are those that have no moving parts, as opposed to mechanical banks which move in some way. Over 200 collectors from all over America, Canada and Europe arrived for the event. A Saturday morning auction augmented with open-room trading and visits to local collections were the order for the three-day affair. During one of the presentations, founding member William Werbell recalled the first convention in Hightstown, New Jersey, in 1968, attended by only 23 members. He was amazed at how the club had grown to over 450 members in 25 years.

At the same convention we met David Weingarten and his collecting partner Margaret Majua. They were busy combing the penny banks displayed in each room to acquire new treasures for their growing collection, numbering today over 2000 miniature buildings. Keeping track of their collection requires a computerized data base.

David and Margaret are typical of the new breed of collectors that have developed in the last decade.

Steve and Marilyn Steckbeck recently hosted the Mechanical Bank Collectors of America (MBCA) convention. Participants were treated to carefully designed display cases depicting the complete history of mechanical banks. One case was filled with the entire line of the Shepard Hardware & Mfg. Co., while another case contained all of Steve's favorite banks. They know the history of each piece and have preserved their knowledge on a 28-minute video entitled *The Steckbeck Collection*. Steve and Marilyn are collectors who are responsible for preserving mechanical banks produced during the golden age of America's industrialization.

In the quest to find the banks to present in this study, many fine collections throughout America were visited. Ralph Dye has shared the wonderful variety of ceramic, lead, and cast iron pieces that he has collected for the last 28 years. Another group of unusual banks featured, each with a story, belong to Harold and Rona Blau. Harold, who has a Ph.D. in anthropology, applies his skills as a museum research ethnologist to the study of banks. To him, "toy banks represent ideas from many cultures and time periods." Harold and Rona were collectors when they met; now they happily search for banks together, sharing their knowledge with other collectors by producing articles for the SBCCA's *Penny Bank Post* magazine.

Joe Eichler agreed to bring a number of his tin and dime register banks to last year's SBCCA convention. Brian Cleary, Gerald Lange, Tom Kellogg, Tom Stoddard, Carl White and Dick Soukup allowed me to study special banks in their collections. Many of the photographs of the silver, silver plated, and lead banks were provided by Thomas Lautz, Director of the Museum of History of Money, in Cologne, Germany.

Don Duer
Winter Park, Florida
June, 1996

CONTENTS

FOREWORD

Benjamin Franklin wrote in the late 18th century, "The way to wealth is as plain as the way to market; it chiefly depends on two words: industry and frugality." Much later, in the mid-19th century, Abraham Lincoln's wisdom emerged when he told his peers to, "Teach economy, that is one of the first virtues, it begins with saving money." Walter P. Chrysler, the automobile manufacturer and early collector of mechanical banks, whose legendary collection was sold in the 1950s, said that next to the tool box from his days as a journeyman machinist, he valued most his elaborate collection of toy banks. The concept of thrift has been instilled in children throughout history. Most youngsters are familiar with the phrase, "A penny saved is a penny earned." These early statesmen who spoke of thrift had no idea of the significance toy banks would have in today's collecting world; not so much for the pennies saved, but for the value of the penny banks themselves.

In order to provide a way to save money, local craftsmen during the late 1700s and early 1800s fabricated a variety of small penny banks from clay, tin and wood. Hawkers and walkers loaded hand-crafted banks on their backs with other household items and distributed them to homes and businesses. It wasn't until the mid-19th century that J. & E. Stevens began earnestly manufacturing a line of cast iron toy banks. The Stevens' factory, located in Cromwell, Connecticut, became the cradle of the toy bank industry in America. Old timers remember the factory situated on Nook's Hill Road in a valley called Frog Hollow, named for thousands of croaking frogs in a pond adjacent to the foundry. At the Stevens' site, some of the original buildings are still in place. Fol-

lowing the Civil War, new foundries of industrialization turned toy banks out by the wagon loads. With an average markup of a few cents per bank, a first run of 10,000 pieces was needed to assure profit. Between 1869 and 1939, thousands of different toy banks were designed and produced. It is these banks that collectors eagerly search for to enhance their collections.

Using this book

Over 1,600 penny banks, from a number of well-known collections, are organized into eight chapters grouped by type (such as mechanical and pocket banks) or by material (like cast iron, ceramic and tin). Within each chapter, sub-groupings, like people and animals, make identification of a particular bank easier. Insight is given to the wide variety of collectible banks that can be found in major collections throughout the world.

Each numbered **bank caption** includes the **name of the bank**, **height in inches** to the nearest one eighth inch, **country of origin**, **date of manufacture** and **bank rating guide**. For those pieces that have never been pictured, a new name was assigned. In some cases the manufacturer or material are noted.

Rating banks is a complex task particularly subject to bias. Most collectors tend to give the highest ratings to banks that they own. Ratings are often influenced by unusually high prices set in auctions and in antique market places. For this study, the ratings were based solely on the availability of the bank to the collector. Over the years the availability of banks may change, therefore affecting their rating.

BANK RATING GUIDE:

A - Common Banks: found in many locations and collections.

B - Unusual Banks: commonly found in antique shops and shows.

C - Exceptional Banks: hard to find except in good collections.

D - Scarce Banks: seldom found except in better collections.

E - Rare Banks: few are known to exist except in advanced collections.

F - Invaluable Banks: only a handful are known to exist.

A values reference is at the back of the book. Here a range of values is given for each of the different rating guides within each chapter. The reference is based on the current market value, taking into account the number of banks available, their condition, color and desirability. Obviously, nearly mint specimens command much higher values than average banks of the same type. The value guide is just that, a guide, and not an absolute document. Its interpretation is subject to the discretion of the seller and buyer and the laws of supply and demand.

CHAPTER 1

CAST IRON

If a poll of penny bank collectors were taken, a majority probably would say that cast iron banks are their favorites. The production of cast iron still banks began soon after the American Civil War when iron foundries turned their output to making domestic items to fill the needs of a growing economy. Because the factories had geared up for war, there was an abundance of surplus iron and a large number of foundry workers looking for work. Carl White recently found a patent drawing No. 46,779 dated March 14, 1865 issued to Benjamin Cole for a *Money Safe* in the shape of a building that registers the coins put in the bank. The earliest still bank patent was issued to Abram and George Wright in 1869 for the *Puzzle Try Me* safe bank. Since these modest beginnings thousands of cast iron penny banks have been manufactured.

Manufacturing process

Once a designer had come up with an idea for a new bank, he would make a drawing and secure a patent to protect the idea from competitive manufacturers. Next, skilled pattern makers would translate the design into a wood or metal pattern. The pattern was usually made in two or more parts and mounted on a plate. Next, a loose fitting wood or metal box called a flask was placed around the pattern and damp clay/sand was tamped in firmly to fill all voids. The patterns were carefully removed from the flask leaving a hollow mold. Openings called gates were made for allowing molten iron to be poured into the mold. When the iron had cooled the casting was removed from the flask, cleaned, filed and polished. In the finishing room the banks were nickel plated, electroplated, japanned or hand painted by artists called strippers. The pieces were then ready for final assembly and packing for shipment to the vendor.

Competition promotes variety

There were many manufacturers producing cast iron banks in the mid-nineteenth century. In 1869, J. & E. Stevens began to manufacture *Hall's Excelsior* mechanical and *Lilliput* still banks. In 1874, Smith & Egge under contract with Ives, Blakeslee & Co. began producing the *Boston State House*, *Masonic Temple* and *Moody and Sankey* banks. By 1876 the Enterprise Manufacturing Co. of Philadelphia came out with the *Independence Hall* and *Tower* banks for the Centennial Exposition. Kyser & Rex, a foundry just outside Philadelphia in Frankford, introduced the *Apple, Kneeling Camel, Globe Savings Fund* and a number of beautiful safe banks in 1882. Early in the 1890s, the Kenton Hardware Co. in Ohio produced the *Columbia* series of still banks for the Columbian World Exposition in Chicago. Later they would produce such famous banks as the *Flat Iron Building, Statue of Liberty, Bank of Industry* and *Crosley Radio*. From 1902 to 1909, John Harper patented 15 banks, including the famous American president portrait safes, manufactured by the Chicago Hardware Foundry. Between 1910 and 1920, the Arcade Manufacturing Co. of Freeport, Illinois, had created the *Eggman* and *Arcade Steamboat* banks. During this same period A. C. Williams introduced the *Aunt Jemima, Clown Bank* and *Two Faced Indian*. No history of cast iron penny bank production would be complete without mentioning such great companies as the Hubley Manufacturing Co. of Lancaster, Pennsylvania; the Judd Manufacturing Co. of Wallingford, Connecticut; and the Grey Iron Casting Company of Mount Joy, Pennslyvania, which later was purchased by the John Wright Co. of Wrightsville, Pennsylvania. In England, Sydenham & McOustra and Chamberlain & Hill competed for the European market for cast iron banks.

Each of these foundries was responsible for the huge number of cast iron penny banks that emerged in the late 19th and early 20th centuries. This period can be considered the Golden Age of cast iron penny bank production.

Today, only a few individuals and companies design and produce a limited number of cast still banks for collectors. The future of penny bank manufacturing in the United States seems assured, though, largely through the interest of an industrial arts teacher in Falls Church, Virginia.

Charles Reynolds designed and produced his first still bank, the *Amish Man*, in 1980. He casts his banks in aluminum in a small foundry on his property. To date, he has produced over 60 types of still banks. Reynolds carries on the tradition of earlier bank designers such as Charles Bailey, George Brown, Russel Frisbie and John Hall.

Those who are drawn to cast iron still banks are looking for specimens that exhibit a lot of original color and are undamaged. They are displayed as examples of a rare, nearly lost art. The reader is directed to the large number of cast iron still banks shown in the books *The Penny Bank Book* by Andy and Susan Moore and *A Penny Saved, Still and Mechanical Banks* by this author. This work includes a limited number of unusual color variations and pieces which have been seldom published.

1 Officer, 5-3/4", American, Hubley, c. 1910, **D.**

2 Sailor, 5-1/2", American, Hubley, c. 1910, **C.**

3 Baseball Player, 5-3/4", American, A. C. Williams, c. 1920, **D.**

4 Clown, 6-1/4", American, A. C. Williams, c. 1910, **A.**

5 Aunt Jemima, 5-7/8", American, A. C. Williams, c. 1920, **B.**

6 Give Me A Penny, 5-5/8" American, Wing, c. 1894, **C.**

7 Dolphin, 4-1/2", American, Gray Iron, c.1900, **D.**

8 Dutch Boy On Barrel, 5-5/8", American, Hubley, c.1930, **A.**

9 Dutch Girl Holding Flowers, 5-1/4", American, Hubley, c. 1930, **A.**

10 Two-Faced Black Boy, 3-1/8", American, A. C. Williams, c. 1910, **B.**

11 Eggman, 4-1/8", American, Arcade, c. 1910, **E.**

12 Buster Brown & Tige, 5-1/2", American, A. C.Williams, c. 1920, **C.**

13 Two Faced Indian, 4-1/4",
American, A. C. Williams, c. 1905,
E.

14 Taft-Sherman (Back), 4",
American, J. M. Harper, c. 1908, **D.**

15 Mulligan-Benny & Fish (Front),
5-3/4", American, Hubley, c. 1920,
D.

16 Mulligan-Benny & Fish (Back),
5-3/4", American, Hubley, c. 1920,
D.

17 Monkey With Hat, 4-1/8",
American, Unknown, c. 1930, **E.**

18 Hippo, 2-5/8", American, Unknown, c. 1920, **E.**

19 Rooster, 4-5/8", American, Arcade, c. 1910, **B.**

20 Bird On Stump, 4-3/4", American, A. C. Williams, c. 1915, **D.**

21 Chanticleer, 4-5/8", American,
Unknown, c. 1911, **F.**

22 Spitz, 4-1/4", American, Gray Iron, c. 1928, **D.**

23 Horse With Band, 4-1/4", American, Unknown, c. 1915, **D**

24 Squirrel With Nut, 4-1/8", American, Unknown, c. 1915, **D.**

25 Rabbit On Base, 2-1/4", American, Unknown. c. 1884, **E.**

26 Good Luck Horseshoe, 4-1/4", American, Arcade, c. 1910, **B.**

27 Labrador Retriever, 4-1/2", American, Unknown, c. 1920, **D.**

28 Jumbo Soap Elephant, 3", American, Unknown, c. 1925, **D.**

29 Hairy Buffalo, 3", American, Unknown, c. 1920, **C.**

30 Murphy Rotary Pig, 3", American, A. C. Williams, c. 1910, **D.**

31 Possum, 2-3/8", American, Arcade, c. 1910, **D.**

32 Rhino, 2-5/8", American, Arcade, c. 1910, **F.**

33 Honey Bear, 2-1/2", American, Unknown, c. 1910, **E.**

34 Begging Bear, 5-3/8", American, A. C. Williams, c. 1910, **B.**

35 Lion On Wheels, 4-1/2", American, A. C. Williams, c. 1920, **C.**

36 Begging Rabbit, 5-1/8", American, A. C. Williams, c. 1908, **B.**

37 Koala Bear, 4-1/2", American, Unknown, c. 1930, **D.**

38 Nesting Hen, 4", American, Unknown, c. 1930, **D.**

39 I'm From Missouri Mule, 4", American, Unknown, c. 1930, **D.**

40 I Hear A Call, 5", American, Unknown, c. 1900, **C.**

41 Bluebird, 4-1/4", American, Unknown, c. 1920, **D.**

42 Steer On Base, 4-1/4", American, Unknown, c. 1930, **E.**

43 Seated Hippo, 3-3/4", American, Unknown, c. 1930, **C.**

44 Man In Barrel, 3-3/4", American, J. & E. Stevens, c. 1890, **D.**

45 Van Dusen Pig, 2-1/4", American, Unknown, c, 1930, **D.**

46 Walking Bear, 2-3/4", American, Unknown, c. 1910, **F.**

47 Decorated Horse On Tub, 5-3/8" American, A. C. Williams, c. 1920, **C.**

48 Two Kids, 4-1/2", American, Unknown, c.1910, **D.**

49 Circus Elephant, 3-3/8", American, Hubley, c. 1930, **B.**

50 Prancing Horse, 4-1/4", American, Arcade, c. 1910, **B.**

51 Porky Pig, 5-3/4", American, Hubley, c. 1930, **C.**

52 Boston Bull, Seated, 4-1/4", American, Hubley, c. 1930, **C.**

53 Terrier, Seated, 4-5/8", American, Hubley, c. 1930, **C.**

54 Art Deco G.O.P. Elephant, 4", American, Unknown, c. 1930, **C.**

55 Small Elephant, 3", American, Arcade, c. 1910, **B.**

58 Alphabet, 3-7/8", American, Unknown, c. 1900, **E.**

56 Chicken Feed Bag, 4-5/8", American, Knerr, c. 1973, **B.**

57 Pig With Bow, 3", American, Shimer, c. 1899, **C.**

59 Car Load Of Cash, 1-3/4", American, Unknown, c. 1920. **F.**

60 $100,000 Money Bag, 3-5/8",
American, Unknown, c. 1920, **D.**

61 Checker Cab, 4-1/4", American,
Arcade, c. 1921, **D.**

62 Statue Of Liberty On Bell,
8-1/2" American, Unknown, c. 1926,
E.

63 Statue Of Liberty, 9-5/8",
American, Wing, c. 1900, **C.**

64 San Gabriel Mission, 4-5/8",
American, Unknown, c. 1906, **F.**

65 State Bank, 5-7/8", American,
Gray Iron, c. 1895, **E.**

66 State Bank, 6-1/8", American,
Kenton, c. 1900, **D.**

67 New Bank, 5-1/4", American,
J.& E. Stevens, c. 1872, **E.**

68 Triangular Building, 6",
American, Hubley, c. 1914, **D.**

69 Tower Bank, 6-7/8", American, Kyser & Rex, c. 1890, **D.**

70 Westminster Abbey, 6-3/8", England, Sydenham & McOustra, c. 1908, **B.**

71 Masonic Temple, 6-1/4", American, Smith & Egge, c. 1874, **F.**

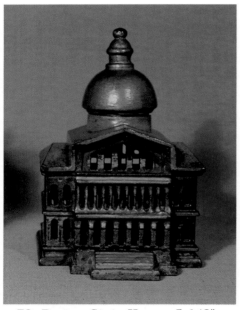

72 Boston State House, 5-1/8", American, Smith & Egge, c. 1874, **E,**

73 City Bank With Chimney, 6-3/4", American, Unknown, c. 1873, **E.**

74 Home Savings Bank, 5-7/8", American, J. & E. Stevens, c. 1896, **C.**

75 Crown Bank On Legs, 4-7/8", American, Smith & Egge, c. 1875, **E.**

76 House with Bay Window, 4-7/8", American, Unknown, c. 1882, **D.**

77 Town Hall Bank, 4-5/8", American, Kyser & Rex, c. 1882, **D.**

78 Moody & Sankey, 5", American, Smith & Egge, c. 1870, **E.**

79 Recording Administration Building, 6-3/4", American, Unknown, c. 1891, **F.**

80 Park Bank, 4-3/8", American, Penn, c. 1880, **E.**

81 Columbia Bank, 4-1/2", American, Kenton, c. 1893, **E.**

82 Oval Bank, 3", American, Kyser & Rex, c. 1880, **D.**

83 Lilliput, Still, 4-1/2", American, J. & E. Stevens, c. 1875, **E.**

84 Pagoda Bank, 5", England, Unknown, c. 1889, **D.**

85 Domed Mosque, Combination, 5-1/8", American, Gray Iron, c. 1903, **C.**

86 Bank With Bell, 7-1/2", Austrian, Unknown, c. 1900, **E.**

87 Pavilion, 3-1/8", American, Kyser & Rex, c. 1880, **D.**

88 Skyscraper With Clock, 5-3/8", American, A.C. Williams, c. 1910, **E.**

89 Crown Bank, 3-5/8", American, J. & E, Stevens, c. 1875, **C.**

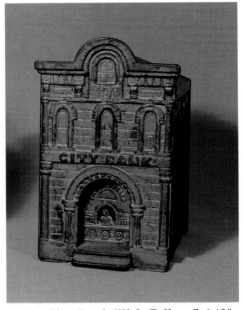

90 City Bank With Teller, 5-1/2", American, H. L. Judd, c. 1880, **C.**

91 Pearl Street Bank, 4-1/4", American, Unknown, c. 1900, **E.**

92 Masonic Temple, 4-3/4", American, Smith & Egge, c. 1874, **F.**

93 Saving Bank, 5-7/8", American, Unknown, c. 1880, **E.**

94 Finial Bank, 5-3/4", American, Kyser & Rex, c. 1887, **D.**

95 Home Bank with Crown, 5-1/4", American, J. & E. Stevens, c. 1872, **C.**

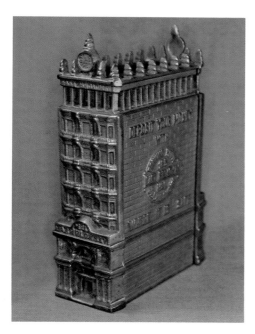

96 Jarmulowsky Building, 7-3/4', American, C. G. Shepard, c. 1910, **D.**

97 Ironmaster's House, Combination, 4-1/4", American, Kyser & Rex, c. 1884, **D.**

98 Bird Bank On Legs, 6-1/2", France, Unknown, c. 1900, **E.**

99 Lichfield Cathedral, 6-1/2", England, Chamberlain & Hill, c. 1908, **D.**

100 Savings Deposit, 3-7/8", American, Star, c. 1900, **D.**

101 Childrens Safe Deposit, 4-1/8", American, J .& E. Stevens, c. 1929, **B.**

102 Daisy Safe Deposit, 3-5/8", American, Arcade, c. 1902, **C.**

103 Church Window Safe, 2-7/8", American, Unknown, c. 1890, **B.**

104 Fidelity Safe, 2-1/2", American, Kyser & Rex, c. 1880, **E.**

105 Circle Door Safe, 2-1/2",
American, Unknown, c. 1890, **D.**

106 Treasure Safe, 5", American,
J. & E. Stevens, c. 1897, **B.**

107 Czar Safe, 3-3/8",
American, Arcade, c. 1902, **C.**

108 National Safe, 4-7/8",
American, Arcade, c. 1902, **B.**

109 Horsehead Safe, 5-1/2",
American, Kenton, c. 1911, **D.**

110 Stenciled Door Safe, 4-1/4",
American, Unknown, c. 1880, **C.**

111 State Savings Bank, No. 358,
4-7/8", American, Nicol, c. 1895, **D.**

112 Security Safe, 5-1/8",
American, Unknown, c. 1890, **D.**

113 Indian Cent Safe, 3-3/8",
American, Unknown, c. 1880, **C.**

114 The Bank of Industry,
5-3/8", American, Gray Iron, c.
1903, **C.**

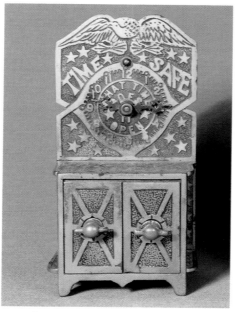

115 Time Safe, 7-1/8",
American, E. M. Roche, c.1900, **D.**

116 Security Safe, 4-1/2",
American, Unknown, c. 1894, **B.**

117 Pet Safe, 4-1/2",
American, Kenton, c.1900, **C.**

118 Arched Door Safe, 4-1/4",
American, Unknown, c. 1881, **D.**

119 National Safe, Eagle, 4-1/8",
American, Unknown, c. 1880, **D.**

120 Arched Door Safe, 4-1/4",
American, Unknown, c. 1881, **D.**

121 The Keyless Safety, Deposit,
5-7/8", American, Keyless Lock, c.
1890, **C.**

122 Stenciled Door Safe, 4-1/4",
American, Unknown, c. 1880, **C.**

123 The Home Bank, 6-1/2", American, Wing, c. 1900, **D.**

124 Horn Of Plenty, 4", American, E. M. Roche, c. 1900, **F.**

125 Rosette Safe, 4", American, Unknown, c. 1890, **B.**

126 Sure Luck, 5-1/2", American, E. M. Roche, c. 1885, **F.**

127 Cupid Safe, 4-3/4", American, Kenton, c. 1911, **C.**

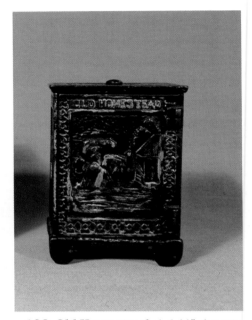

128 Old Homestead, 4-1/4", American, Shimer, c. 1899, **E.**

129 Save Your Pennies, 3-1/2", American, Kenton, c. 1915, **C.**

130 Moon And Star Safe, 5", American, Unknown, c. 1890, **D.**

131 U.S. Navy Bank, 3-3/8", American, Arcade, c. 1902, **D.**

132 Columbian Safe Deposit,
2-3/4", American, Unknown, **D.**

133 Savings For Deposit, 2-3/4",
American, Unknown, c. 1915, **F.**

134 The Globe, 5-3/8",
American, Kenton, c. 1915, **B.**

135 Three Dial Safe, 5-1/4", American, Unknown, c. 1890, **F.**

136 Baby/Stork Safe, 5-5/8",
American, J. M. Harper, c. 1907, **D.**

137 Santa With Pack Safe, 4-1/8",
American, J. M. Harper, c. 1907, **E.**

138 Washington Bust Safe, 6",
American, J. M. Harper, c. 1907, **E.**

139 The Best/Clothing, 4",
American, Regent, c. 1900, **E.**

140 Safe Deposit, 3-5/8",
American, Shimer, c. 1899, **B.**

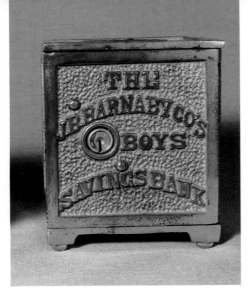

141 J.B. Barnaby/Boys Saving,
4-1/2", American, Unknown, c.
1900, **E,**

142 Floral Safe, 4-5/8", American,
J. & E. Stevens, c. 1898, **C.**

143 Egyptian Safe, 4-5/8", American, Kyser & Rex, c. 1882, **D.**

144 Paul Jones, 3-3/8",
American, Shimer, c.1895, **E.**

145 Tennis Safe, 3", American,
Shimer, c. 1899, **F.**

146 Gem Security Safe, 3-3/8",
American, Unknown, c. 1890, **F.**

147 Puzzle Try Me, 2-1/2",
American, Unknown, c. 1868, **E.**

148 Hexagonal Door Safe, 4",
American, Klotz, c. 1910, **C.**

149 Hexagonal Door/Grill, 4-3/8",
American, Klotz, c. 1910, **D.**

150 Red Ball Safe, 3", American, Unknown, c. 1925, **C.**

151 White City Puzzle Safe No.12, 4-3/4", American, Nicol, c. 1893, **C.**

152 Royal Safe Deposit, 5-7/8", American, Unknown, c. 1890, **C.**

153 Jewel Safe, 5-1/4", American, Unknown, c. 1900, **D.**

154 The Daisy Safe, 2-1/4", American, Unknown, c. 1900, **D.**

155 U.S. Army / Navy Bank, 6-1/8", American, Kenton, c. 1900, **D.**

156 Home Safety Bank, 3-7/8", American, Unknown, c. 1920, **F.**

157 Jewel Safe w/Grille, 7-5/8", American, J. & E. Stevens, c. 1907, **D.**

159 National Safe Deposit, 5-7/8", American, Ives, c. 1897, **C.**

160 Safe Deposit, 5-1/4", American, Hart, c. 1890, **C.**

158 Star Safe, 3-1/2", American, Unknown, c. 1905, **A.**

161 The Mint Safe, 4-5/8",
American, Unknown, c. 1930, **E.**

162 Ideal Bank, 6-3/8",
American, Unknown, c. 1920, **C.**

163 Sampson Safe, 5-1/4", American, Arcade, c. 1900, **F.**

164 Four Posted Safe, 4-3/4",
American, Unknown, c. 1900, **C.**

165 Bank Of Columbia, 5", American, Arcade c. 1891, **C.**

166 Coin Bank, 4-1/4", American, J. & E. Stevens, c. 1905, **C.**

169 G.E. Refrigerator, 3-3/4", American, Hubley, c. 1930, **A.**

170 Satchel, Wright Banking, 3-1/2", American, Unknown, c. 1920, **C.**

167 Liberty Bell, 1905, 3-3/4",
American, J. M. Harper, c. 1905, **D.**

168 Liberty Bell/Yoke, 3-1/2",
American, Arcade, c. 1925, **A.**

171 Gem Stove, 4-1/4", American, Abendroth, c. 1910, **C.**

172 U.S. Mail, 3-1/2", American, A. C. Williams, c. 1915, **C.**

173 Air Mail Bank/Base, 6-3/8", American, Dent, c. 1920, **C.**

174 Save Your Pennies, 6", American, Unknown, c. 1900, **C.**

175 Street Clock, 6", American, A. C. Williams, c. 1920, **D.**

176 Ornate Hall Clock, 5-7/8", American, Hubley, c. 1915, **D.**

177 Standing Mailbox, 5-1/2", American, Hubley, c. 1928, **C.**

178 Grandfather's Clock, 5-5/8", England, Unknown, c. 1910, **F.**

179 Champion Heater, 4-1/8", American, Unknown, c. 1930, **C.**

182 Fortune Ship, 4-1/8",
England, Unknown, c. 1910, **E.**

180 Fidelity Trust Vault, 4-7/8",
American, J. Barton Smith, c. 1890,
D.

181 Red Cross Ship, 4-1/8",
American, Unknown, c. 1910, **F.**

185   Toy Radio Bank, 2-3/4",
American, J. & E. Stevens, c. 1920,
E.

186 Crosley Radio, 4-3/8",
American, Kenton, c. 1931, **C.**

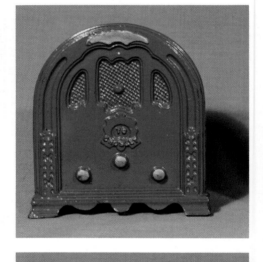

183   Maine, Large, 5-1/4", American, Grey Iron, c. 1897, **E.**

184 Radio with Combination Door,
4-1/2", American, Kenton, c. 1936,
A.

187 U.S.A. Liberty Tank, 3",
American, Unknown, c. 1916, **C.**

188 Coca Cola Vending Bank, 3-
3/4", American, Unknown, c. 1934,
F.

189 Canon, 3", American, Hubley,
c. 1914, **E.**

190 Sun Dial, 4-1/2", American, Arcade, c. 1910, **E.**

191 Water Wagon, 3-1/2", American, Unknown, c. 1930, **D.**

192 Junior Cash Register, 4-1/4", American, J. & E. Stevens, c. 1915, **B.**

193 Rocking Chair, 6-3/4", American, Unknown, c. 1898, **E.**

194 Piano Bank, 5-3/4", American, E. M. Roche, c. 1900, **E.**

195 Old Volunteer F.D. Bank, 5", American, Unknown, c. 1910, **E.**

96 Stop Sign, 5-5/8", American, Dent, c. 1920, **C.**

197 Fire Alarm, 4-1/4", Japan, Unknown, c. 1930, **D.**

198 Baseball Bank, 2-3/4", American, Hubley, c. 1915, **E.**

199 Basket Of Corn, 2-1/4", American, J. M. Harper, c. 1907, **E.**

200 Urn, 4-1/4", American, Unknown, c. 1890, **D.**

201 Thy Kingdom Come Book, 2-3/4", German, Unknown, c. 1900, **E.**

202 Globe On Hand, 4", American, Unknown, c. 1893, **E.**

203 Columbia Saving Bank, 5-3/4", American, Unknown, c. 1881, **E.**

204 Apollo Bank, 4-1/4", American, Wright, c. 1968, **A.**

205 Union Dime Savings, 3-3/4", American, c. 1882, **E.**

206 Beehive On Base, 4-1/8", England, Harper, c. 1897, **E.**

207 1879 Silver Dollar, 3", American, Unknown, c. 1879, **D.**

CHAPTER 2

CERAMICS

Since only a few ceramic banks exhibit pottery marks, little has been written about ceramic bank manufacturers. Many of the banks were made in war-torn countries where records of their manufacture have been destroyed. Researchers are digging into the histories of the Staffordshire factories in England, the Frie Onnaing factories of France, the Roseville factories of America, and Austrian, German, Japanese and other ceramic factories throughout the world.

Ceramic banks were hand formed or cast from clay, glazed and fired in a kiln. Older banks do not show the mold marks because careful attention was given to remove any joint in the bank before it was glazed. Later production pieces exhibit the mold marks since speed became important in order to fill the demand for the bank.

Although fragile, ceramic banks depict both historical and humorous aspects of the countries from which they emerged. Ceramic penny banks were considered expedient and hence were often broken by children in utter frustration while attempting to retrieve coins inside the bank. Small chips, especially around coin slots, affect the bank's value. Collectors sometimes overlook the chips if the bank is a rare specimen or one of a kind. Within the chapter we described the various types of banks you will encounter in hopes that you can appreciate their colorful beauty.

Earthenware Banks

One of the earliest known low-fired earthenware banks was found in an excavation of a Grecian temple in the village of Thessalia in the eastern part of present day Turkey. The *Thesaurus Bank* (meaning "treasury") was made in the shape of a small temple complete with a door and ornamented pediment. It is remarkable that the bank survived for over 2,500 years; grave robbers have broken most of these early banks while searching for the silver and gold they contained.

Dating from the Roman Empire, 500 B.C. to 400 A.D., earthenware banks in the shape of a woman's breast have been excavated by archeologists. The breast form was thought to be a symbol of bounty. Other unglazed banks from this period have been found in the forms of animals, beehives, bowls and chests.

Most of the earliest earthenware banks were handmade with coils and slabs of clay, pinching and molding them into the desired shape. Later ceramic banks were produced by throwing a wedge of clay onto a moving wheel and hand pulling and manipulating the clay into a closed container shape. The coin slots were usually cut into the sides of the piece before decorative slips were applied.

Earthenware banks were made in Austria from the mid-19th century until the 1930s. Each beautiful piece is covered with colorful translucent glazes in green, yellow, blue and rose hues. The number inscribed or stamped into the base refers to a pattern number, not the date of production.

Stoneware Banks

Banks were made of clay and fusible stone by local potteries in America and England in the 1600s. The white, gray and brown clay bodies were decorated with painted motifs and usually covered with a salt glaze.

Porcelain Banks

High-fired porcelain banks first appeared in Holland about 1650 when potters there tried to duplicate the Chinese porcelain objects they acquired in trade from Asia. The bowl and vase shaped banks were hand painted and glazed with floral and oriental designs.

Delft Banks

During this same period, blue and white tin glazed (called delftware after the Dutch city of Delft) banks were made in Holland and later in England, again to try to duplicate Chinese wares.

Redware Banks

Typically American, redware clay banks were produced in potteries from New England to Georgia from the 1700s to well into the 20th century. Redware's color comes from traces of iron oxide found in the clay, which when fired produces the red body hue. Colored slips were applied to decorate the simply shaped folk art pieces. Redware Banks were molded into jugs, barrels, animals, heads, fruit and vegetables. Few good banks have survived the ravages of use over the years. A type of decorated redware called "Jaspe" was produced in the Alsace region of France from 1700 to 1930. Its distinguishing feature is a mottled, layered glaze. Many of the banks are bulbous shaped.

Yellow ware Banks

From 1830 to the 1920's, yellow ware banks were manufactured in America. The yellow color of each piece varied slightly due to its position within the kiln during firing.

Spongeware Banks

At the same period, spongeware banks emerged in England. They were decorated by dabbing blue, brown and green glazes on the clay body using a sponge. Also during this period, a similar ware but with brown mottled glaze from Rockingham, England, were produced as banks. Often these pieces are mistaken for a similar-looking ware made in Bennington, Vermont.

Staffordshire Banks

In the early 19th century, banks were being produced in Staffordshire, England, from hard, somewhat translucent clay and fired at high temperatures to form porcelain. They were carefully crafted and artistically painted. Many Staffordshire banks were cast in molds using a slurry to speed production.

Majolica Banks

Made in England, Austria, and Czechoslovakia from about 1860 to the 1930s are majolica banks. Majolica banks primarily took the form of faces or figures. Each earthenware glazed piece is unique in the way the artist combined the green, rose, yellow, blue, brown and turquoise glazes.

Japanese Banks

Most of the banks made in Japan during the 1930s are hand painted on a white porcelain body. If they are stamped "Made in Occupied Japan", they were made between 1947 and 1953.

208 Boy/Bandanna, 3-1/2", Austrian, Majolica, c. 1900, **E.**

209 Dutch Girl, 3-3/8", Austrian, Majolica, c. 1900, **D.**

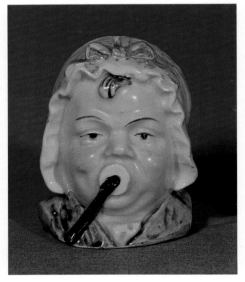

210 Baby/Pacifier, 3-1/4", Austrian, Majolica, c. 1900, **C.**

211 Boy/Purple Hat, 3-1/4",
Austrian, Majolica, c. 1900, **C.**

212 Clown/Top Hat, 3-1/2",
Austrian, Majolica, c. 1900, **E.**

213 Clown/Jester, 3-5/8",
Austrian, Majolica, c. 1900, **D.**

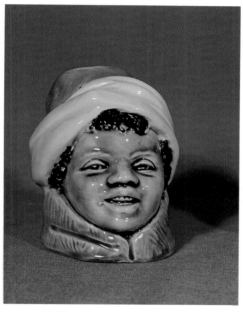

214 African/Turban, 3-1/8",
Austrian, Majolica, c. 1900, **D.**

215 Plains Indian, 3-7/8",
Austrian, Majolica, c. 1900, **C.**

216 Smiling Man/Cap, 3-3/8",
Austrian, Majolica, c. 1900, **D.**

217 Dapper Man/Cigar, 3-5/8",
Austrian, Majolica, c. 1900, **D.**

218 Boy/Baseball Cap, 3-5/8",
Austrian, Majolica, c. 1900, **E.**

219 Woman/Headband, 3-1/4",
Austrian, Majolica, c. 1900, **C.**

220 Pig/Cigar, 2-7/8",
Austrian, Majolica, c. 1900, **E.**

221 Cartoon Head, 3-1/8",
Austrian, Majolica, c. 1900, **E.**

222 Cartoon Head, 3-1/8",
Austrian, Majolica, c. 1900, **E.**

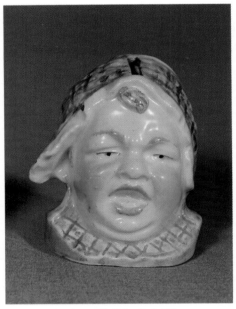

223 Crying Child, 3-1/2",
Austrian, Majolica, c. 1900, **C.**

224 Man/Pink Hat, 3-3/8",
Austrian, Majolica, c. 1900, **D.**

225 Woman/Bonnet, 3-5/8",
Austrian, Majolica, c. 1900, **D.**

226 Puzzled Man/Purple Hat, 3-
1/2", Austrian, Majolica, c. 1900, **E.**

227 Man/Green Hat, 3-1/4",
Austrian, Majolica, c. 1900, **F.**

228 Blond Man/Blue Hat, 3-1/4",
Austrian, Majolica, c. 1900, **F.**

229 Smiling Man/Red Hat,
3-1/4", Austrian, Majolica, c. 1900,
E.

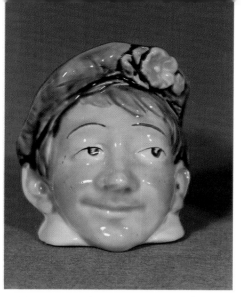

230 Man/Flower Cap, 3-3/8", Austrian, Majolica, c. 1900, **D.**

231 Jester/Blue Hat, 3-3/4", Austrian, Majolica, c. 1900, **E.**

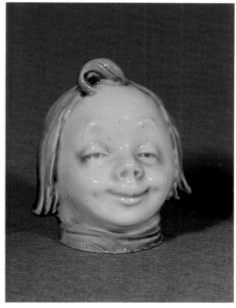

232 Boy/Blond Hair, 3-1/4", Austrian, Majolica, c. 1900, **E.**

233 Woman/Feather Hat, 3-3/4", Austrian, Majolica, c. 1900, **D.**

234 Old Man/Cap, 3-1/4", Austrian, Majolica, c. 1900, **E.**

235 Man/Brown Hat, 3-5/8",
Czechoslovakia, Majolica, c. 1930, **C.**

236 Woman/Bonnet, 3-3/4",
Czechoslovakia, Majolica, c. 1930, **D.**

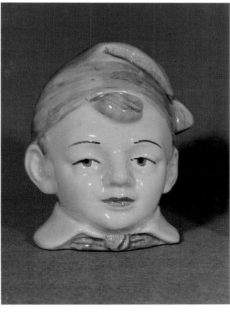

237 Boy/Brown Cap, 3-3/4",
Czechoslovakia, Majolica, c. 1930, **C.**

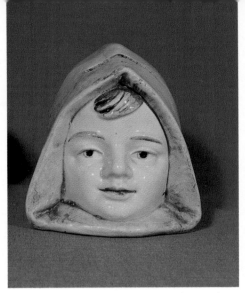

238 Woman/Hood, 3-1/2", Czecho-slovakia, Majolica, c. 1930, **C.**

239 Woman/Hood, 3-1/8", Aus-trian, Majolica, c. 1900, **D.**

240 Scottish Man/Cap, 3/14", Unknown, Majolica, **D.**

241 Clown/Pointed Cap, 3-1/2", Unknown, Porcelain, c. 1880, **F.**

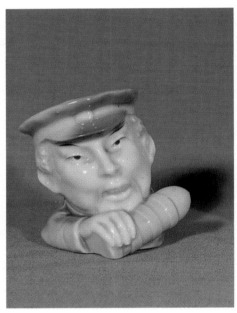

242 Officer/Shell, 3", Austrian, Porcelain, c. 1920, **E.**

243 Child/Hood, 3-1/2", Austrian, Porcelain, c. 1930, **D.**

244 Smiling Black, 2-3/4", Ameri-can, Redware, c. 1870, **E.**

245 Mexican/Hat, 3-3/8", Aus-trian, Stoneware, c. 1920, **E.**

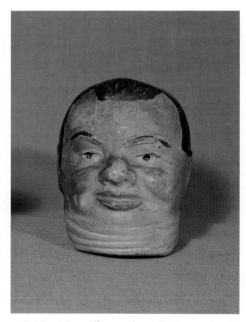

246 Man/Receding Hair, 3-5/8", Austrian, Stoneware, c. 1920, **E.**

247 Seaman/Pipe, 2-5/8", Austrian, Stoneware, c. 1920, **D.**

248 Monk Head, 3-3/4", Austrian, Stoneware, c. 1920, **F.**

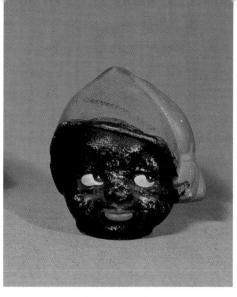

249 Black Boy/Blue Cap, 3", American, Porcelain, c. 1930, **D.**

250 Oriental Man, 3-1/4", Japan, Porcelain, c. 1930, **C.**

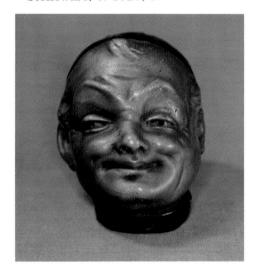

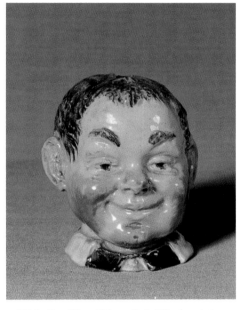

251 Smiling Man, 3-1/2", Austrian, Stoneware, c. 1930, **D.**

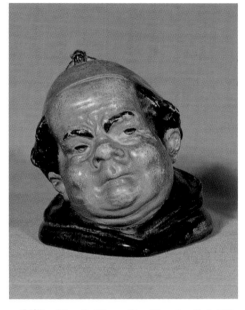

252 Monk/Bee On Head, 3-1/2", Spain, Stoneware, c. 1880, **F.**

253 Foxy Grandpa, 3-1/4", American, Earthenware, c. 1870, **E.**

254 Smiling Man, 3", Austrian, Porcelain, c. 1930, **C.**

255 Boy/Green Cap, 3", Austrian, Stoneware, c. 1930, **D.**

256 Scotsman, 4-1/2", Austrian, Stoneware, c. 1915, **E.**

257 Band Leader, 6-1/4", Austrian, Porcelain, c. 1910, **D.**

258 Charles Stuart Rex, 5", Austrian, Porcelain, c. 1910, **E.**

259 Black Woman/Wall Hanger, 5", American, Earthenware, c. 1940, **D.**

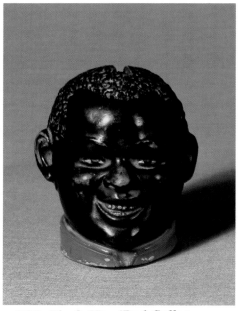

260 Black Man/Red Collar, 3-3/4", American, Redware, c. 1880, **E.**

261 Black Man/Wall Hanger, 5-1/2", Mexican, Earthenware, c. 1940, **D.**

262 Girl/Scarf, 3-1/2", Austrian, Stoneware, c. 1920, **C.**

263 Uncle Sam, 4-1/4", American, Stoneware, c. 1900, **E.**

264 Chinaman/Mammy, 3-1/4", Austrian, Stoneware, c. 1885, **E.**

265 Policeman/Mustache, 3-3/4", Austrian, Stoneware, c. 1930, **E.**

266 Uncle Sam, 4-1/4", American, Stoneware, c. 1900, **E.**

267 Smiling Monk, 2-5/8", Austrian, Stoneware, c. 1930, **C.**

268 Happy Hooligan, 3", Austrian, Stoneware, c. 1920, **D.**

269 Oriental Man, 2-7/8", Austrian, Stoneware, c. 1920, **D.**

270 Keystone Cop, 3-1/4", Austrian, Stoneware, c. 1920, **D.**

271 Dutch Girl, 3-3/8", Austrian, Stoneware, c. 1930, **C.**

272 Thin Man/Hat, 3-1/2", Austrian, Stoneware, c. 1930, **D.**

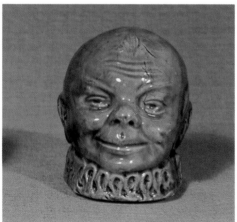

273 Clown, 2-3/4", Austrian, Stoneware, c. 1930, **D.**

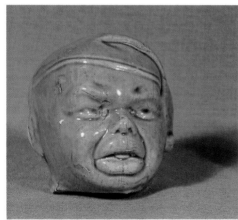

274 Grumpy Man, 2-7/8", Austrian, Stoneware, c. 1900, **C.**

275 Boy/Cap, 2-3/4", Austrian, Stoneware, c. 1900, **E.**

276 Napoleon Man, 3-1/4", England, Stoneware, c. 1900, **E.**

277 Man/Bow Tie, 3-3/4", England, Rockingham, c. 1920, **D.**

278 Punch, 3", France, Stoneware, c. 1920, **D.**

279 Fritz, 3-1/2", Austrian, Stoneware, c. 1920, **D.**

280 Smiling Black Face, 2-3/4", American, Redware, c. 1875, **D.**

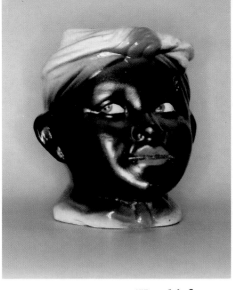

281 Black Woman/Kerchief, 4-1/2", American, Raku, c. 1890, **C.**

282 Black Woman/Necklace, 6-1/2", England, Chalkware, c. 1920. **D.**

283 Funny Face Boy, 3", German, Stoneware, c.1930, **D.**

284 Fukusuke, 3-1/8", Japan, Porcelain, c. 1930, **D.**

285 Painted Face, 2-1/4", Mexican, Earthenware, c. 1930, **D.**

286 Black Mask, 3-3/4", American, Redware, c. 1885, **D.**

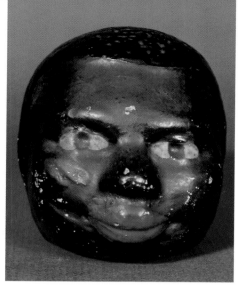

287 Black Face/Lips, 3", American, Chalkware, c. 1900, **D.**

288 Man On Moon, 2-3/4", American, Redware, c. 1880, **E.**

289 Woman/Green Kerchief, 2-1/8", England, Staffordshire, c. 1890, **D.**

290 Colonial Statesman/Grey Cap, 2-1/8", England, Staffordshire, c. 1890, **D.**

291 Colonial Woman/Hat, 2-1/8", England, Staffordshire, c. 1890, **E.**

292 Colonial Man/White Hat, 2-1/8", England, Staffordshire, c. 1890, **E.**

Left:
293 Colonial Man/Brown Hat, 2-1/8", England, Staffordshire, c. 1890, **E.**

296 Colonial Statesman/Red Cap, 2-1/8", England, Staffordshire, c. 1890, **D.**
297 Scottish Man/Cap, 2-1/2", England, Porcelain, c. 1900, **D.**

294 Colonial Man/Black Hat, 2-1/8", England, Staffordshire, c. 1890, **E.**

Left:
295 Frowning Woman, 2-1/4", England, Staffordshire, c. 1890, **E.**

298 Spaniel Head, 2-1/8", England, Staffordshire, c. 1890, **E.**

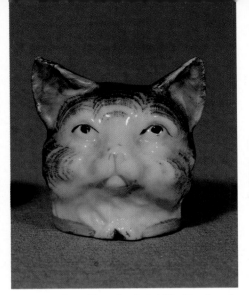

299 Cat Head, 2-1/8", England, Staffordshire, c. 1890, **D.**

300 Ram Head, 2-1/4", England, Staffordshire, c. 1890, **E.**

301 Sheep Head, 2-1/4", England, Staffordshire, c. 1890, **E.**

302 Man/Top Hat, 2-1/2", German, Porcelain, c. 1880, **D.**

303 Woman/Hat, 2-5/8", German, Porcelain, c. 1880, **D.**

304 Royal Guard, 6", Austrian, Porcelain, c. 1915, **D.**

305 Mountain Regiment, 5-1/2", Austrian, Porcelain, c. 1915, **D.**

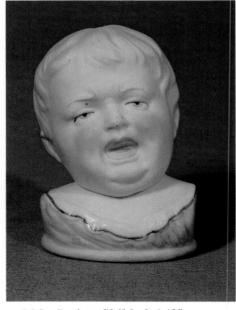

306 Crying Child, 3-1/2", German, Porcelain, c. 1890, **D.**

307 Brewmaster, 3-1/4", German, Porcelain, c. 1930, **C.**

308 Child/Dog On Sofa, 2", German, Porcelain, c. 1925, **D.**

309 Boy/Sealed Letter, 3-1/4", German, Porcelain, c. 1925, **D.**

310 Man On Moneybag, 3-3/4", England, Porcelain, c. 1920, **C.**

311 Boy Riding Pig, 3-3/4", German, Porcelain, c. 1900, **E.**

312 Man/Money Sacks, 4", German, Porcelain, c. 1930, **D.**

313 Boy On Plaid Bag, 2-3/4", German, Porcelain, c. 1930, **C.**

314 Boy Feeding Pig, 3-1/2", German, Porcelain, c. 1900, **E.**

315 Imp Playing Flute, 3-1/4", German, Porcelain, c. 1900, **E.**

316 Girl With Ball, 5-3/4", Austrian, Majolica, c. 1900, **D.**

317 Girl/Money Box, 3-1/2", German, Porcelain, c. 1900, **E.**

318 Boy With Spoon, 5", Austrian, Majolica, c. 1900, **D.**

319 Lady/Chest, 3-1/2", England, Porcelain, c. 1900, **D.**

320 Man/Pouch, 3-1/2", England, Porcelain, c. 1900, **E.**

321 Boy/Basket, 3-1/2", Austrian, Porcelain, c. 1900, **E.**

322 Boy With Box, 3", England, Porcelain, c. 1900, **C.**

323 Angel/Heart, 3", German, Porcelain, c. 1920, **E.**

324 Running Boy/Chicken, 4", German, Porcelain, c. 1925, **F.**

325 Child In Egg, 2-3/4", German, Porcelain, c. 1880, **E.**

326 Girl In Egg, 3-3/8", Austrian, Porcelain, c. 1900, **D.**

327 Man/Time Is Money, 4", German, Porcelain, c. 1930, **C.**

328 Child On Potty, 3-5/8", Austrian, Porcelain, c. 1930, **C.**

329 Two Children, 3-5/8", Austrian, Porcelain, c. 1930, **D.**

330 Brunette Child/Basket, 2-1/2", German, Porcelain, c. 1925, **D.**

331 Blond Child/Basket, 2-1/2", German, Porcelain, c. 1925, **D.**

332 Monk, 4-3/8", German, Porcelain, c. 1930, **E.**

333 Child On Apple, 3", Austrian, Porcelain, c. 1900, **D.**

334 Kneeling Soldier/Rifle, 5-1/2", Austrian, Porcelain, c. 1930, **C.**

335 Man/Chair, 7-1/2", German, Chalkware, c. 1925, **C.**

336 Black Boy/Watermelon, 4-1/4", German, Porcelain, c. 1930, **C.**

337 Sailor, 6", Austrian, Earthenware, c. 1920, **D.**

338 Santa Claus, 5", Austrian, Earthenware, c. 1900, **D.**

339 Humpty Dumpty, 4-3/4", American, Earthenware, c. 1920, **D.**

340 Man With Stick, 7-1/2", Austrian, Earthenware, c. 1900, **D.**

341 Seated Man with Chickens, 6", Austrian, Earthenware, c. 1925, **D.**

342 Fat Man Resting, 5-1/4", Austrian Earthenware, c. 1900, **D.**

343 Mulligan On Egg, 4-1/2", Austrian, Earthenware, c. 1900, **D.**

344 Merry Xmas Santa/Bag, 5", Austrian, Earthenware, c. 1900, **C.**

345 Happy Hooligan Standing, 5-7/8", Austrian, Earthenware, c. 1900, **B.**

346 Happy Hooligan/Egg, 4-5/8", Austrian, Earthenware, c. 1900, **D.**

347 Clown, 5-1/4", Austrian, Earthenware, c. 1900, **C.**

348 Boy On Egg, 4-1/4", Austrian, Earthenware, c. 1900, **D.**

349 Jack In Box, 4-5/8", Austrian, Earthenware, c. 1900, **B.**

350 Grumpy Gus, 5-3/8", Austrian, Earthenware, c. 1900, **B.**

351 Three Children/Bag, 3-7/8", Austrian, Earthenware, c. 1900, **D.**

352 Baby In Basket, 4-1/2", Austrian, Earthenware, c. 1920, **D.**

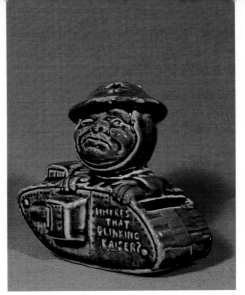

353 Tommy In Tank, 3-3/4", England, Earthenware, c. 1917, **C.**

354 Happy Hooligan/Barrel, 4-1/2", Austrian, Earthenware, c. 1920, **C.**

355 Crying Baby/Tub, 3-3/4", American, Earthenware, c. 1930, **D.**

356 Girl With Flowers, 4", Austrian, Earthenware, c. 1920, **C.**

357 Mushroom Man, 3-1/8", Austrian, Earthenware, c. 1930, **E.**

358 Dutch Boy, 5", German, Redware, c. 1930, **C.**

359 Man/Trench Coat, 4-7/8", Austrian, Porcelain, c. 1930, **B.**

360 Dutch Girl, 5", German, Redware, c. 1930, **C.**

361 Dog/Chair, 6-1/4",
American, Porcelain, c. 1950, **C.**

362 Man/Trench Coat, 4-1/8",
Austrian, Earthenware, c. 1900, **C.**

363 John Howard, 8-3/4",
American, Porcelain, c. 1950, **B.**

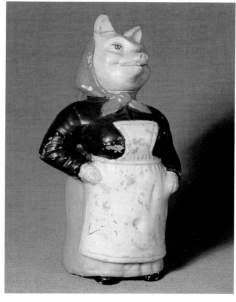

364 Pig/Apron, 6", German, Earthenware, c. 1930, **D.**

365 Middy Bank, 5-1/4", American,
Redware, c. 1930, **D.**

366 Shakespearean Man, 5-3/4",
Austrian, Majolica, c. 1900, **F.**

367 St. Claus, 5", American, Earthenware, c. 1900, **F.**

368 Fat Man/Bow Tie, 2-1/4",
German, Porcelain, c. 1930, **C.**

**369 Emperor Joseph & Kaiser
Wilhelm,** 3-5/8", England, Parian
Ware, c. 1912, **E.**

370 Mexican/Cactus, 4",
Japan, Porcelain, c. 1950, **A.**

371 Preacher/Pulpit, 4-1/8",
Austrian, Porcelain, c. 1930, **C.**

372 Mexican/Suitcase, 3",
Japan, Porcelain, c. 1950, **A.**

373 Thin Indian Chief, 4-1/8",
Japan, Porcelain, c. 1950, **A.**

374 Indian/Headdress, 3-7/8",
Japan, Porcelain, c. 1950, **A.**

375 Squaw, 3-1/8",
Japan, Porcelain, c. 1950, **B.**

376 Girl/Collection Box, 5-1/8",
German, Goebel, c. 1975, **C.**

377 Monk/Pitcher, 5-1/8",
England, Porcelain, c. 1950, **C.**

378 Seaman, 5-1/2", American,
Earthenware, c. 1950, **B.**

379 Elephant/Saddle, 3-7/8", Austrian, Porcelain, c. 1930, **D.**

380 Begging Spaniel, 4-5/8", Austrian, Majolica, c. 1900, **D.**

381 Dog With Pipe, 4-1/2", Austrian, Majolica, c. 1900, **D.**

382 Cat With Bow, 4-1/4", Austrian, Earthenware, c. 1930, **C.**

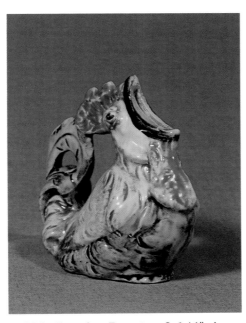

383 Crowing Rooster, 3-1/4", Austrian, Majolica, c. 1900, **F.**

384 Peacock, 5", Austrian, Majolica, c. 1900, **D.**

385 Parrot On Stump, 4", Austrian, Majolica, c. 1890, **F.**

386 Elephant, 1-7/8", Austrian, Porcelain, c. 1920, **D.**

387 Rabbit/Cabbage, 3-1/8", England, Majolica, c. 1900, **F.**

388 Cat/Hat, 4-1/4", Austrian, Earthenware, c. 1900, **D.**

389 Dog/Hat, 4-1/4", Austrian, Earthenware, c. 1900, **D.**

390 Dog Head, 3", Austrian, Earthenware, c. 1920, **C.**

391 Poodle Head, 2-1/2", Austrian, Earthenware, c. 1920, **C.**

392 Cat Head, 2-3/4", Austrian, Porcelain, c. 1930, **D.**

393 Terrier Head, 3-1/4", Austrian, Earthenware, c. 1920, **D.**

394 Monkey Head, 3-1/2", Austrian, Earthenware, c. 1900, **C .**

395 Cat Head, 3-1/8", Austrian, Earthenware, c. 1920, **C.**

396 Frog Head, 2-7/8", Austrian, Earthenware, c. 1930, **C.**

397 Cat Head, 3-3/8", Austrian, Earthenware, c. 1920, **C.**

398 Pointer, 2-1/2", Austrian, Earthenware, c. 1920, **D.**

399 Owl Head, 3", Austrian, Earthenware, c. 1930, **C.**

400 Dog Head, 3", Austrian, Earthenware, c. 1920, **C.**

401 Fox Head, 2-7/8", Austrian, Earthenware, c. 1920, **D.**

402 Elephant, 2-3/8", Austrian, Earthenware, c. 1920, **C.**

403 Eagle Head, 2-1/2", Roseville, Earthenware, c. 1890, **E.**

404 Dog Head, 3-7/8", Roseville, Earthenware, c. 1890, **D.**

405 Cat Head, 4", Roseville, Earthenware, c. 1890, **D.**

406 Chick, 2-3/4", Austrian, Earthenware, c. 1900, **D.**

407 Seated Pig, 3-7/8", Austrian, Yellow ware, c. 1920, **C.**

408 Easter Chick, 3-5/8", Austrian, Earthenware, c. 1900, **E.**

409 Pig/Money Bag, 4-1/2", Austrian, Earthenware, c. 1920, **C.**

410 Chick, 3-1/4", Austrian, Earthenware, c. 1920, **C.**

411 Animal In Egg, 3-5/8", Austrian, Earthenware, c. 1920, **D.**

412 Seated Monkey, 4-7/8", Austrian, Earthenware, c. 1930, **C.**

413 Hen In Basket, 2-7/8", Austrian, Earthenware, c. 1920, **C.**

414 Chick In Shell, 2-3/8", Austrian, Earthenware, c. 1920, **C.**

415 Rabbit With Egg, 5-1/2",
Austrian, Earthenware, c. 1900, **E.**

416 Two Dogs In Basket, 3",
Austrian, Earthenware, c. 1900, **C.**

417 Seated Cat, 3-7/8",
Austrian, Earthenware, c. 1920, **F.**

418 Possum In Carriage, 3-3/4",
Austrian, Earthenware, c. 1900, **E.**

419 Rabbit Lying Down, 2-1/4",
American, Redware, c. 1900, **E.**

420 Cat In Bag, 3-3/4",
Austrian, Earthenware, c. 1920, **C.**

421 Pig In Purse, 2-3/4",
Austrian, Earthenware, c. 1930, **C.**

422 Animal Cart, 2-3/4",
Austrian, Earthenware, c. 1900, **E.**

423 Honey Bear, 3-1/2",
Austrian, Earthenware, c. 1930, **C.**

424 Pig In Bag, 3-3/8",
Austrian, Earthenware, c. 1930, **B.**

425 Rooster, 2-1/2", French,
Yellow ware, c. 1880, **E.**

426 Elephant, 3-7/8", Austrian,
Earthenware, c. 1930, **B.**

427 Large Pig, 4", Austrian,
Earthenware, c. 1920, **D.**

428 Small Pig, 3-1/4", Austrian,
Earthenware, c. 1920, **D.**

429 Pig In Purse, 3-1/4", Austrian,
Earthenware, c. 1900, **C.**

430 Rabbit Lying Down, 2-5/8",
Austrian, Earthenware, c. 1900, **D.**

431 Mountain Goat, 2-1/2",
Austrian, Earthenware, c. 1900, **C.**

432 Resting Pig, 2-3/8",
Austrian, Earthenware, c. 1920, **C.**

433 Seated Bulldog, 4-1/2",
American, Earthenware, c. 1930, **D.**

434 Kneeling Lamb, 3-3/4",
Austrian, Earthenware, c. 1900, **D.**

435 Sleeping Pig, 6-1/2" l.,
German, Earthenware, c. 1920, **E.**

436 Seated Cat, 4", American,
Redware, c. 1879, **F.**

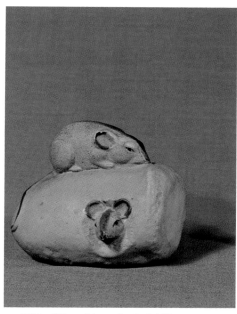

437 Mice/Bread, 2-3/8",
Austrian, Earthenware, c. 1930, **E.**

438 Cat In Basket, 3-1/2",
American, Redware, c. 1880, **D.**

439 Seated Bear, 4-3/8",
American, Earthenware, c. 1900, **F.**

440 Duck, 2-7/8",
Austrian, Earthenware, c. 1920, **E.**

441 Owl On Rock, 4",
Austrian, Earthenware, c. 1920, **E.**

442 Pig In Jar, 3-1/2", Japan, Porcelain, c. 1930, **C.**

443 Polar Bear, 2-1/2", Japan, Porcelain, c. 1930, **B.**

444 Rabbit/Egg, 3-3/8", Czech. Earthenware, c. 1930, **C.**

445 Begging Dog, 3-3/8", Austrian, Porcelain, c. 1930, **C.**

446 Dog/House, 3", German, Porcelain, c. 1930, **D.**

447 Pig/House, 3", Austrian, Porcelain, c. 1930, **D.**

448 Van Dyke Tea Rabbit, 3-1/2", England, Earthenware, c. 1930, **C.**

449 Sleeping Dog, 2-3/4", German, Earthenware, c. 1900, **D.**

450 Fat Pig, 3", Czech. Porcelain, c. 1935, **B.**

451 Seated Elephant/Locket, 3-1/4", German, Porcelain, c. 1930, **D.**

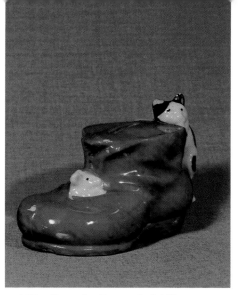

452 Cats In Boot, 2-1/2", German, Porcelain, c. 1930, **C.**

453 Swan, 2-5/8", German, Porcelain, c. 1925, **E.**

454 Dog In Egg, 2-1/2", German, Porcelain, c. 1900, **D.**

455 Cats In Bag, 3-7/8", German, Porcelain, c. 1930, **E.**

456 Dog On Chair, 2-5/8", England, Staffordshire, c.1900, **E.**

457 Monkey/Bag, 3-1/2", German, Porcelain, c. 1930, **D.**

458 Bear Holding Cub, 4-1/2", Austria, Majolica, c. 1930, **B.**

459 Dog With Pouch, 5-1/2", Austrian, Majolica, c.1930, **E.**

460 Bear/Locked Egg, 3-5/8",
Austrian, Porcelain, c. 1930, **C.**

461 Performing Bear, 3-5/8",
Austrian, Porcelain, c. 1930, **B.**

462 Performing Bear, 3-3/4",
Czechoslovakia, c. 1930, **C.**

463 Basset Hound Seated, 3-5/8",
Austrian, Porcelain, c. 1930, **D.**

464 Dog With Pouch, 5-1/2", Austrian, Porcelain, c. 1930, **C.**

465 Dog In House, 2-3/4", Austrian, Porcelain, c. 1930, **C.**

466 Standing Dog, 3-3/4",
Austrian, Porcelain, c. 1930, **B.**

467 Seal, 3", Austrian, Porcelain, c. 1930, **C.**

468 Ocelot/Ball, 4-1/4", Austrian, Porcelain, c. 1930, **D.**

469 Parrot, 4", Japan, Porcelain, c. 1930, **C.**

470 Toucan, 4-1/8", Japan, Porcelain, c. 1930, **C.**

471 Pelican, 4-1/8", Japan, Porcelain, c. 1930, **C.**

472 Big Eyed Dog, 4-3/4", Japan, Porcelain, c. 1930, **A.**

473 Big Eyed Dog, 3", Japan, Porcelain, c. 1930, **B.**

474 Happy Dog, 2-3/4", Japan, Porcelain, c. 1930, **A.**

475 Dog/Dog House, 2-7/8", Japan, Porcelain, c. 1930, **B.**

476 Dog/Peddle Cart, 2-7/8", Japan, Porcelain, c. 1930, **C.**

477 Dog With Mandolin, 4-1/8", Japan, Porcelain, c. 1930, **B.**

478 Bulldog Face, 3-1/8", Japan, Porcelain, c. 1930, **C.**

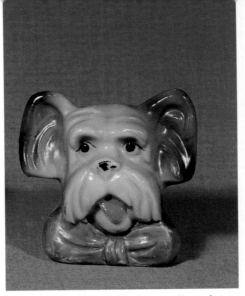

479 Dog Face, 3", Japan, Porcelain, c. 1930, **C.**

480 Pig Face, 3-1/8", Japan, Porcelain, c. 1930, **C.**

481 Black Eyed Scottie, 4-7/8", Japan, Porcelain, c. 1930, **B.**

482 Black Scottie, 3", Japan, Porcelain, c. 1930, **B.**

483 Alert Scottie, 4-1/8", Japan, Porcelain, c. 1935, **B.**

484 Scottie In Doghouse, 3-3/4", Japan, Earthenware, c. 1930, **C.**

485 Hand's Off Dog, 4-1/2", Japan, Redware, c. 1930, **C.**

486 Dog With Cigar, 5", Japan, Earthenware, c. 1935, **C.**

487 Tropical Fish, 3-1/2", Japan, Porcelain, c. 1930, **D.**

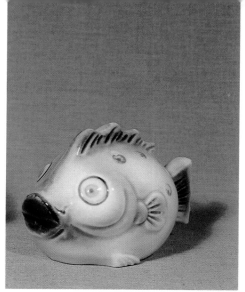

488 Small Fish, 2-1/2", Japan, Earthenware, c. 1950, **B.**

489 Tired Horse, 3-1/4", Japan, Porcelain, c. 1930, **B.**

490 Mule With Bags, 3-1/2", Japan, Porcelain, c. 1935, **B.**

491 Mule With Bags, 3-1/4", Japan, Porcelain, c. 1935, **A.**

492 Smallest Piggy Bank, 1-5/8", Japan, Porcelain, c. 1935, **C.**

493 Pig With Money, 2", German, Porcelain, c. 1925, **D.**

494 Ireland Pig, 2-7/8", England, Earthenware, c. 1930, **C.**

495 Pig/Flowers, 2-1/4", Austria, Earthenware, c. 1900, **D.**

496 Happy Pig, 4-5/8", Japan, Porcelain, c. 1930, **B.**

497 Mr. Pig, 4-3/8", Japan, Earthenware, c. 1950, **B.**

498 Mrs. Pig, 4-3/8", Japan, Earthenware, c. 1950, **B.**

499 Decorated Pig, 4-1/2", Japan, Earthenware, c. 1930, **C.**

500 Pig/Accordion, 4-3/8", Japan, Porcelain, c. 1930, **C.**

501 Pig In Formal, 4-1/4", Japan, Earthenware, c. 1930, **B.**

502 Thin Pig, 3-1/8", American, Earthenware, c. 1950, **B.**

503 Copley Pig, 4-3/8", American, Earthenware, c. 1950, **B.**

504 Farmer Pig, 4-3/4", Japan, Porcelain, c. 1930, **C.**

505 Oriental Elephant, 3-1/2",
Japan, Porcelain, c. 1930, **B.**

506 Panda Bear, 2-5/8",
Japan, Porcelain, c. 1930, **B.**

507 Art Deco Cat/Ball, 4-1/4",
Japan, Earthenware, c. 1930, **C.**

508 Chinese Dragon Fish, 4-3/8",
Chinese, Porcelain, c. 1930, **D.**

509 Standing Owl, 3-1/2", Japan,
Porcelain, c. 1930, **B.**

510 Owl Head, 2-1/2",
Japan, Porcelain, c. 1930, **B.**

511 White Owl, 4",
Japan, Porcelain, c. 1950, **A.**

512 Owl/Large Eyes, 4-5/8",
Japan, Porcelain, c. 1935, **B.**

513 Baby Owl, 3-1/2",
Japan, Porcelain, c. 1930, **C.**

514 Pigeon, 4-1/2", France, Majolica, c. 1900, **D.**

515 Brown Bird, 4", American, c. 1880, **D.**

516 Gretel On Swan, 6-1/2", German, Chalkware, c. 1930, **F.**

517 Small Bird, 3-1/4", American, Earthenware, c. 1900, **C.**

518 Chicken On Nest, 2-1/2", American, Earthenware, c. 1900, **C.**

519 Chicken/Handle, 3-1/2", Mexican, Earthenware, c. 1900, **D.**

520 Bird On Sphere, 4-3/4", American, Earthenware, c. 1900, **E.**

521 Cockatoo, 7", France, Porcelain, c. 1900, **C.**

522 Flying Eagle, 5-1/4", American, Earthenware, c. 1875, **D.**

523 Devil On Trunk, 3-1/2", German, Porcelain, c. 1930, **E.**

524 Devil With Hand/Trunk, 4-1/2", German, Porcelain, c. 1930, **D.**

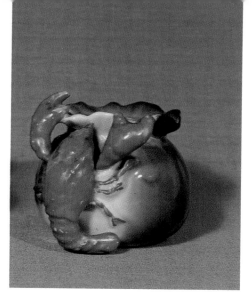

525 Lobster/Bag, 2-1/2", German, Porcelain, c. 1930, **C.**

526 Pig In Drum, 2-5/8", German, Porcelain, c. 1930, **C.**

527 Pig In Bag, 2-3/4", German, Porcelain, c. 1930, **C.**

528 Lobster, 1-5/8", German, Porcelain, c. 1930, **B.**

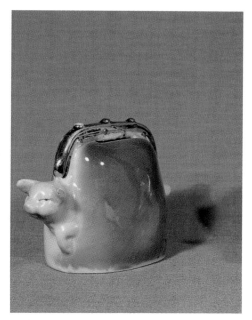

529 Pig In Purse, 2-5/8", German, Porcelain, c. 1930, **B.**

530 Turkey, 4", German, Porcelain, c. 1930, **B.**

531 Dog By Purse, 2-5/8", German, Porcelain, c. 1930, **C.**

532 Bear/Savings Box, 3", German, Porcelain, c. 1930, **D.**

533 Two Pigs/Seesaw, 3-1/8", German, Porcelain, c. 1930, **B.**

534 Bear/Trunk, 2-3/4", German, Porcelain, c. 1930, **C.**

535 Elephant, 3-1/2", Holland, Delftware, c. 1910, **D.**

536 Bear/Mail Box, 3-1/4", German, Porcelain, c. 1930, **D.**

537 Pig By Purse, 3", German, Earthenware, c. 1925, **C.**

538 Donkey, 3-1/2", Austrian, Porcelain, c. 1925, **E.**

539 Dog On Books, 4-1/2", Japan, Earthenware, c. 1930, **C.**

540 Pig Playing Flute, 3-1/8", German, Porcelain, c. 1930, **D.**

541 Dog On Covered Wagon,
3-7/8", American, Earthenware, c.
1920, **E.**

542 Pumpkin Face, Front, 3-1/4",
American, Redware, c. 1885, **F.**

543 Pumpkin Face, Rear, 3-1/4",
American, Redware, c. 1885, **F.**

544 Child In Crib, 3-1/8", European, Earthenware, Reproduction, **B.**

545 Decorated Pig, 2", German,
Porcelain, c. 1930, **C.**

546 Seated Panda, 3-1/4",
Japan, Porcelain, c. 1930, **B.**

547 Monkey/Banana, 6", American, Porcelain, c. 1950, **B.**

548 Buddha, 4-1/2", Japan, Stoneware, c. 1950, **B.**

549 Girl/Umbrella, 6", Japan,
Earthenware, c. 1950, **C.**

550 Victorian House, 4-1/8",
Austrian, Earthenware, c. 1900, **C.**

551 Lover's House, 3-7/8",
Austrian, Porcelain, c. 1900, **D.**

552 Two Chimney House, 3-3/4",
England, Staffordshire, c. 1870, **D.**

553 Chimney House, 3-1/4", England, Staffordshire, c. 1900, **C.**

554 Two Man/House, 4-7/8",
England, Staffordshire, c. 1890, **C.**

555 Red House, 3-7/8",
England, Staffordshire, c. 1890, **C.**

556 Small House, 2-7/8", Austrian,
Earthenware, c. 1925, **C.**

557 Small Cottage, 4-3/4",
England, Staffordshire, c. 1900, **C.**

558 Small House, 2-7/8",
Austrian, Earthenware, c. 1930, **C.**

559 Dutch House, 3-1/2",
Holland, Porcelain, c. 1930, **C.**

560 Cottage Bank, 3-1/8", American, Porcelain, c. 1925, **D.**

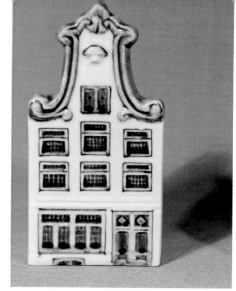

561 Dutch Building, 4-1/2", Holland, Earthenware, c. 1960, **B.**

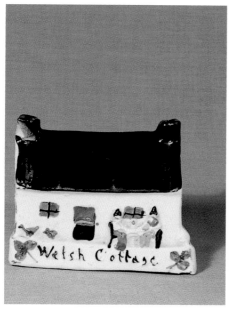

562 Welsh Cottage, 3-3/8", England, Earthenware, c. 1920, **D.**

563 Six Sided Bank, 4-3/8", England, Earthenware, c. 1930, **D.**

564 Red School House, 3", American, Earthenware, c. 1930, **B.**

565 Chickens/House, 3-1/4", Austrian, Porcelain, c. 1930, **E.**

566 Thesaurus Bank, 6-1/4", German, Earthenware, Reproduction, **F.**

567 Little Brown Church, 3-1/2", American, Earthenware, c. 1930, **B.**

568 Apple, 1-3/4", England, Staffordshire, c. 1890, **E.**

569 Pear, 1-3/4", England, Staffordshire, c. 1890, **E.**

570 Walnut/Leaf, 2-3/4", France, Majolica, c. 1900. **D.**

571 Red Apple, 2-3/4", American, Redware, c. 1875, **B.**

572 Pumpkin, 2-1/8", American, Redware, c. 1875, **E.**

573 Pear, 4", American, Redware, c. 1875, **D.**

574 Squash, 2-3/4", France, Earthenware, c. 1920, **C.**

575 Yellow Apple, 2-1/4", American, Earthenware, c. 1890, **C.**

576 Squash, 2-3/4", France, Majolica, c. 1920, **E.**

577 Painted Flower Jug, 4-5/8",
American, Redware, c. 1870, **D.**

578 Jamestown Expo. Jug,
2-3/4", American, Redware, c. 1907,
E.

579 Painted Flower Jug, 4-3/8",
American, Redware, c. 1870, **D.**

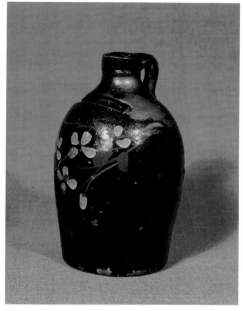

580 Jamestown Expo. Jug,
3-1/4", American, Redware, c. 1907,
E.

581 Redware Jug, 4-1/2",
American, Redware, c. 1880, **C.**

582 A.Y.P. Painted Jug, 2-7/8",
American, Redware, c. 1909, **F.**

583 Bust Form Bank, 3-7/8",
American, Redware, c. 1870, **E.**

584 Pointed Jug, 3-1/2",
American, Earthenware, c. 1870, **F.**

585 Wine Jug, 4-1/8", American,
Redware, c. 1880, **D.**

586 Bust Form Bank, 2-1/2",
American, Yellow ware, c. 1850, **F.**

587 Decorated Bust Form, 3-3/4",
American, Redware, c. 1920, **E.**

588 Jug, 3-1/4", American, Stoneware, c. 1930, **B.**

589 Pointed Jar, 6-1/8", England,
Stoneware, c. 1930, **D.**

590 Agnes Fallick Bank, 4-1/2",
England, Earthenware, c. 1860, **E.**

591 Bank With Handle, 4-1/2",
American, Earthenware, c. 1860, **E.**

592 Glazed Jar, 4-3/4",
France, Jaspe, c. 1880, **D.**

593 Whiskey Jug, 5-1/4",
American, Redware, c. 1870, **E.**

594 Blue Jug, 3-7/8",
American, Stoneware, c. 1925, **D.**

595 Bank Jug, 4-3/8",
American, Stoneware, c. 1900, **E.**

596 Bust Form Bank, 3-5/8",
American, Stoneware, c. 1870, **E.**

597 Savings Bank, 3-7/8",
American, Earthenware, c. 1900, **D.**

598 Savings Jug, 3-1/2",
American, Earthenware, c. 1870, **C.**

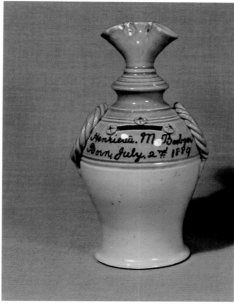

599 Birth Bank, 7-1/4",
England, Earthenware, c. 1887, **E.**

600 Savings Jug, 3",
American, Stoneware, c. 1900, **C.**

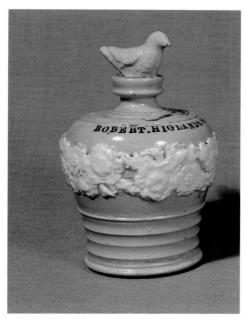

601 Bird/Savings Bank, 6-1/4",
England, Stoneware, c. 1850, **F.**

602 Pointed Jar Bank, 5-1/4",
American, Stoneware, c. 1890, **D.**

603 Spongeware Bank, 2-1/4",
American, Spongeware, c. 1870, **E.**

604 Cash Register, 4-1/8", Austrian, Earthenware, c. 1900, **C.**

605 Deposit Cup, 2-3/4", Austrian, Earthenware, c. 1900, **D.**

606 Piano, 4-1/4", Austrian, Earthenware, c. 1900, **C.**

607 Tree Stump, 3-1/8", Austrian, Earthenware, c. 1900, **D.**

608 Hat/Pipe, 2-7/8", Austrian, Stoneware, c. 1900, **E.**

609 Drum, 2", Austrian, Stoneware, c. 1900, **C.**

610 Decorated Stein, 3-1/2", Austrian, Earthenware, c. 1920, **D.**

611 Mail Box, 3-3/4", Austrian, Stoneware, c. 1900, **B.**

612 C.D. Kenny Co. Stein, 3-3/4", Austrian, Earthenware, c. 1920, **B.**

613 Marvel Safe, 3-1/2",
Austrian, Earthenware, c. 1900, **A.**

614 Siegel Cooper & Co. Safe,
3-1/2", Austrian, Earthenware, c.
1900, **C.**

615 A.D. Mathew & Sons Safe,
3-1/2", Austrian, Earthenware, c.
1900, **E.**

616 Accordion, 3-1/2", Austrian,
Majolica, c. 1900, **C.**

617 Mailbox/Santa Claus, 3-3/4",
Austrian, Earthenware, c. 1900, **C.**

618 Travel Clock, 3-3/8",
Austrian, Earthenware, c. 1900, **D.**

619 Edward Scott Xmas Bank,
3-1/4", American, Earthenware, c.
1887, **F.**

620 Globe, 2-7/8", Austrian, Earthenware, c. 1920, **C.**

621 Trunk, 2-7/8", Austrian,
Earthenware, c. 1920, **A.**

622 Noah's Ark, 3", Austrian, Earthenware, c. 1900, **B.**

623 Funny Car, 2-1/2", Austrian, Earthenware, c. 1930, **D.**

624 Fisherman's Basket, 2-3/8", Austrian, Earthenware, c. 1930, **B.**

625 Suitcase, 2-5/8", Austrian, Earthenware, c. 1920, **C.**

626 Pointed Shoe, 1-7/8", Austrian, Earthenware, c. 1920, **E.**

627 Hat Box, 2-7/8", Austrian, Earthenware, c. 1900, **C.**

628 Woman's Shoe, 2-1/4", Austrian, Earthenware, c. 1900, **D.**

629 Laced Up Shoe, 3-1/4", Austrian, Earthenware, c. 1930, **B.**

630 Child's Shoe, 2-1/2", France, Limoges, c. 1930, **D.**

631 Money Bag, 2-1/2", Austrian, Earthenware, c. 1900, **C.**

632 Purse With Handle, 4", France, Limoges, c. 1880, **F.**

633 Satchel, 2-7/8", Austrian, Earthenware, c. 1925, **B.**

634 Satchel, 2-7/8", Austrian, Earthenware, c. 1925, **B.**

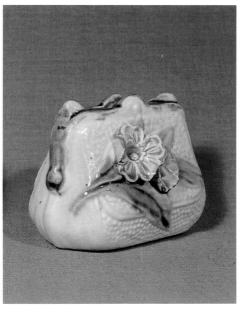

635 Flower Purse, 2-7/8", Austrian, Porcelain, c. 1930, **C.**

636 Flower Purse, 2-7/8", Austrian, Porcelain, c. 1930, **C.**

637 Change Purse, 2-1/2", Austrian, Porcelain, c. 1900, **C.**

638 Bag With Handle, 3", Austrian, Porcelain, c. 1900, **C.**

639 Hat With Flowers, 4", German, Earthenware, c. 1930, **C.**

640 Fruit, 3-1/4", France, Quimper, c. 1930, **E.**

641 Van Dyke Tea Lincoln House, 2-1/2", Austrian, Porcelain, c. 1930, **A.**

642 European Steam Engine, 3", Austrian, Porcelain, c. 1930, **C.**

643 Battleship Maine, 2-3/4", Austrian, Porcelain, c. 1930, **D.**

644 Van Dyke Teapot, 3-1/4", Austrian, Earthenware, c. 1930, **C.**

645 R.B. Bank, 3-3/4", American, Earthenware, c. 1911, **F.**

646 Teapot/Horse, 3-3/4", German, Porcelain, c. 1920, **E.**

647 Teapot/Figures, 2-1/2", German, Jasperware, c. 1920, **E.**

648 Teapot/Figures, 3-3/4", German, Jasperware, c. 1920, **E.**

649 Decorated Heart, 2",
American, Redware, c. 1870, **F.**

650 Fruit In Basket, 2-1/4", American Redware, c. 1900, **C.**

651   Shoe, 2-3/8", American,
Redware, c. 1850, **F.**

652   1K Weight, 3", American,
Redware, c. 1870, **F.**

653   Big Bertha/Drum, 3-1/2",
American, Earthenware, c. 1915, **D.**

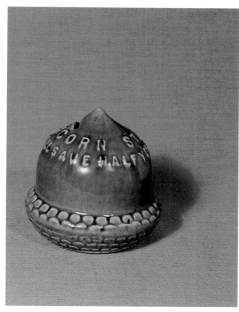

654 Acorn Stoves, 2-7/8",
American, Earthenware, c. 1925, **B.**

655   Clock Tower, 5-1/8", American, Earthenware, c. 1970, **A.**

656   Oriental Fruit, 4-1/8",
Earthenware, c. 1890, **F.**

657 Postal Savings, 4-3/4", American, Earthenware, c. 1950, **B.**

CHAPTER 3

LEAD & WHITE METAL

The beauty of German, French and Japanese lead banks makes these a fast-growing area of collecting interest. Designers from the turn of the century created quantities of pieces in the shapes of animals, birds, buildings, people and ships. Many of the banks sport medallions advertising a historic monument or significant event. Each piece is finely detailed and intricately painted. Some of the banks have hinged heads held together with small hasps and heart-shaped, trick brass locks. Others have small hinged, key locked traps usually mounted on the bottom of the bank.

From 1890 to the 1930s, the company WMF, Wurttembergische Mettalwarenfabrik in Germany, produced a line of lead banks. Intricate metal molds were apparently held together with clamps. Hot lead was poured into the mold and, by using a centrifuge, was forced uniformly into the pattern. The excess lead was evacuated back into a melting pot. After the lead cooled, the hollow bank shell was removed, trimmed, assembled, and sent to the paint shop for final finishing. The metal used in these early banks was almost pure lead with an extremely low melting point. These banks must be handled cautiously for they are extremely fragile and easily damaged. It is very difficult to repair a damaged lead bank because applying heat causes further damage to the bank.

In America, the A. C. Rehberger Company of Chicago, Illinois, was founded in 1912. It produced a fine line of building banks, busts of great men in history, and some novelty banks. Most of the banks were made from the 1920s through the 1960s. Rehberger also jobbed banks for American Art Works and Miller Banking Service.

Another prolific bank manufacturer, Banthrico, was founded in 1931, when Jerome Aronson and Joseph Eisendrath purchased the bankrupt Bankers Thrift Co. Under their leadership Banthrico prospered, making thousands of banks for financial institutions. The banks are made of a zinc aluminum alloy called white metal, composed of 95% zinc and 5% aluminum. Banthrico banks are easily identified by their embossed trap styles which changed shape over the years.

From 1930 to the present, Japanese and other Asian manufacturers produced a number of novelty banks for the American and European markets.

European metal fabricators developed new lines of interesting lead banks from the 1930s to the present. The field of lead bank collecting still needs a considerable amount of research. This is complicated by the fact that so much of the paper history of early fabricators has been destroyed during wars.

Most of the major bank collectors have a few lead pieces on their shelves and interesting stories usually accompany the acquisition of these banks. Lead banks are superb examples of how far designers have taken the craft of producing receptacles for holding our savings. Collectors search for lead banks that are undamaged and exhibit fine detail. In order for a lead bank to have value the paint must be in excellent original condition and not retouched by some enterprising dealer.

The value of lead banks depends on the subject matter, rarity and condition of the bank.

658 Pocahontas Bust, 3-1/8", European, c. 1930, **C.**

659 King Midas/Throne, 5", German, c. 1900, **F.**

660 Frederick of Prussia, 4", German, c. 1912, **D.**

661 Fritz/Empty Pockets, 4", German, c. 1920, **E.**

662 Boy/Top Hat, 4-1/2", German, c. 1920, **E.**

663 Sailor Boy, 4-1/2", German, c. 1910, **E.**

664 Orphan Annie, 4-1/2", German, c. 1910, **E.**

665 Soldier, 6-1/4", German, c. 1920, **E.**

666 Girl/Basket, 4-3/4", German, c. 1920, **F.**

667 Girl/Basket Flowers, 4", German, c. 1925, **D.**

668 Atlas/World, 4-3/4", German, c. 1925, **D.**

669 Pickaninny, 4-1/2", German, c. 1920, **D.**

670 Woodsman, 4-1/4", German, c. 1900, **E.**

671 Soccer Player, 4-1/2", German, c. 1915, **E.**

672 Oriental Santa, 4", Japan, c. 1930, **C.**

673 Seated Mason, 4-1/2", American, c. 1930, **C.**

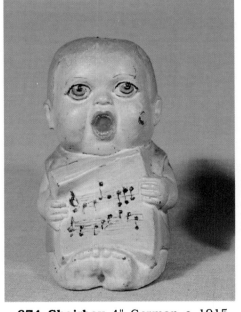

674 Choirboy, 4", German, c. 1915, **E.**

675 Boy On Ball, 6", German, c. 1920, **F.**

676 Daikoku/2 Bags, 4-3/4", Japan, c. 1930, **C.**

677 Man/Sack, 6-1/2", England, c. 1890, **D.**

678 Daikoku/3 Bags, 5-1/2", Japan, c. 1925, **E**

679 Iron Maiden/Square, 4-1/2", German, c. 1920, **E.**

680 Laughing Clown, 3-7/8", German, c. 1910, **E.**

681 Iron Maiden/Round, 4-1/4", German, c. 1920, **F.**

682 Indian Bust, 3-5/8", European, c. 1925, **C.**

683 Indian Chief, 4-1/8", European, c. 1930, **C.**

684 Old Sleepy Eye, 3-1/8", European, c. 1930, **C.**

685 Cat/Ball, 2-1/8", European, c. 1914, **C.**

686 Cat & Dog/Doghouse, 2-7/8", German, c. 1910, **E.**

687 Dog/Tub, 1-3/4", European, c. 1914, **C.**

688 Dutch Girl, 4-1/4", German, c. 1908, **D.**

689 Chimney Sweep, 2-3/8", German, c. 1900, **F.**

690 Old Woman, 4-1/2", German, c. 1925, **C.**

691 Bugs Bunny/Barrel, 5-1/2", American, c. 1940, **A.**

692 Dumbo, 4", American, c. 1930, **C.**

693 Elmer Fudd/Barrel, 5-1/2", American, c. 1940, **A.**

694 Begging Rabbit, 5-1/2", German, c. 1910, **D.**

695 Seated Rabbit, 6", German, c. 1915, **D.**

696 Happy Elephant, 5-1/8", American, c. 1930, **B.**

697 Seated Bulldog, 3-3/4", German, c. 1930, **C.**

698 Elephant, 2-1/2", German, c. 1908, **C.**

699 Dog With Toothache, 4-5/8", German, c. 1925, **E.**

700 Trumpeting Elephant, 4-1/2", German, c. 1908, **D.**

701 Seated Bear, 4-1/4", German, c. 1925, **C.**

702 Dog With Hat, 3-3/8", German, c. 1925, **D.**

703 Dog With Rifle, 4-1/2", German, c. 1920, **D.**

704 Dog With Collar, 4-1/4", German, c. 1920, **D.**

705 Great Northern Goat, 3-1/2", German, c. 1912, **F.**

706 Bear With Top Hat, 5-1/4", German, c. 1910, **F.**

707 Dog/Feathered Cap, 4-3/4", German, c. 1920, **E.**

708 Seated Cat, 3-3/4", German, c. 1920, **E.**

709 Seated Cat, 4-1/4", German, c. 1920, **C.**

710 Seated Gorilla, 4-1/8", American, c. 1930, **B.**

711 Cat With Bow, 4-1/8", German, c. 1930, **D.**

712 Bear/Feathered Cap, 6-1/4", German, c. 1920, **E.**

713 Cat With Bow & Hat, 4-5/8", German, c. 1925, **D.**

714 Bird, 4-1/4", German, c. 1925, **D.**

715 Dog With Pipe, 4", German, c. 1920, **D.**

716 Cat Head, 3-3/8", German, c. 1925, **C.**

717 Cat/Roller-skate, 4-1/4", German, c. 1920, **F.**

718 Elves/Tree Stump, 3-1/4", German, c. 1925, **F.**

719 Seated Cat, 4", German, c. 1925, **F.**

720 Bulldog With Pipe, 3", German, c. 1925, **D.**

721 Dog With Hurt Paw, 5", German, c. 1920, **D.**

722 Bear Family, 3", German, c. 1920, **F.**

723 Standing Hippo, 4-1/2", German, c. 1920, **E.**

724 Parrot, 4", German, c. 1930, **C.**

725 Begging Spaniel, 4-3/8", German, c. 1920, **D.**

726 Dog, 3-3/4", German, c. 1920, **C.**

727 Parrot Head, 3", German, c. 1930, **D.**

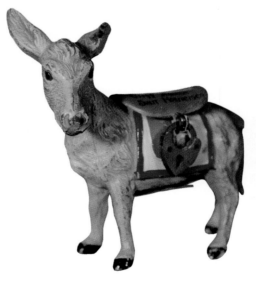

728 Donkey With Saddle, 4", German, c. 1920, **C.**

729 Dachshund, 2-1/2", German, c. 1920, **C.**

730 Donkey/Drum, 3-1/2", German, c. 1930, **D.**

731 Rabbit Sitting, 4-1/2", American, c. 1930, **C.**

732 Tree Stump, 2-1/2", German, c. 1925, **C.**

733 Trumpeting Elephant, 5-1/4", American, c. 1930, **C.**

734 Owl/Book, 4-1/8", German, c. 1925, **F.**

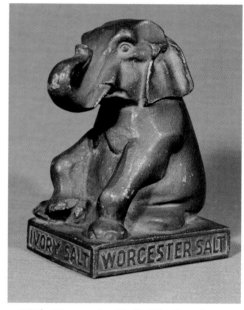

735 Worcester Salt Elephant, 4-1/4", American, c. 1935, **C.**

736 Cat With Toothache, 4", German c. 1925, **D.**

737 Cinnamon Bear, 4", American, c. 1930, **C.**

738 Bear Sitting, 3-3/4", German, c. 1930, **D.**

739 Hen On Nest, 3-7/8", German, c. 1925, **D.**

740 Seated Dog, 5-1/2", American, c. 1935, **C.**

741 Rabbit, 3-3/8", American, c. 1935, **C.**

742 Seated Pig, 4-3/8", American, c. 1935, **B.**

743 Seated Bear, 4-1/2", American, c. 1935, **C.**

744 Bulldog, 4", American, c. 1935, **C.**

745 Elephant/Howdah, 5-1/2", German, c. 1920, **E.**

746 Oriental Elephant, 3-5/8", German, c. 1920, **D.**

747 Seated Frog, 3-1/2", German, c. 1900, **D.**

748 Swan, 2-1/4", Japan, c. 1935, **D.**

749 Parrot, 3-3/4", German, c. 1930, **D.**

750 Mooing Cow, 4-3/8", German, c. 1930, **D.**

751 Parrot, 4-1/4", German, c. 1920, **E.**

752 Bulldog, 3-5/8", England, c. 1930, **D.**

753 Reindeer On Rock, 5", German, c. 1925, **E.**

754 Reclining Dog, 2-5/8", German, c. 1930, **D.**

755 Trumpeting Elephant, 5", American, c. 1935, **C.**

756 Horsehead, 3-1/4", Japan, c. 1935, **C.**

757 Art Deco Cat/Bow, 5-1/2",
American, c. 1930, **C.**

758 Fish, 4", German, c. 1900, **F.**

759 Scotties/Basket, 4-1/2",
American, c. 1930, **A.**

760 Scottie Sitting, 4", German,
c. 1930, **C.**

761 Penguin, 4-3/4", America, c.
1920, **D.**

762 Fox, 3-3/4", German, c. 1925,
D.

763 Seated Pug, 2-3/4", German,
c. 1930, **C.**

764 Cat Playing Piano,
2-1/8", European, c. 1910, **F.**

765 Cat/Toothache, 4", European,
c. 1930, **C.**

766　Man On Drum, 4-3/4", German, c.1930, **D.**

767　Bird/Sailboat, 4-1/4", German, c. 1900, **C.**

768　Fatman Drinking, 4-3/4", German, c. 1900, **E.**

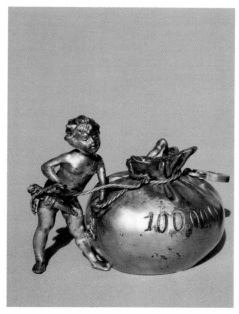

769　Elf/Money Bag, 2-7/8", German, c. 1880, **D.**

770　Dog/Trunk, 3-1/8", German, c. 1900, **D.**

771　Boy Under Mushroom, 4-3/4", German, c. 1875, **F.**

772　Keg Beer/Man, 4-1/8", German, c. 1900, **C.**

773　Man/Monument, 3-1/4", German, c. 1900, **C.**

774　Dog/Monument, 4-3/8", German, c. 1900, **E.**

775 Man/Keg Beer, 4-3/8", German, c. 1900, **C.**

776 Floral Bell, 6-1/8", France, c. 1850, **F.**

777 Man/Keg Beer, 5", German, c. 1900, **D.**

778 Bee/Bee Hive, 3-5/8", German, c. 1900, **B.**

779 Seated Rabbit, 3-3/4", German, c. 1900, **E.**

780 Beehive, 4-3/4", German, c. 1875, **B.**

781 Dog In Doghouse, 2-3/4", France, c. 1900, **C.**

782 Dog/Helmet, 4-3/4", German, c. 1885, **D.**

783 Two Dogs/House, 3-3/4", German, c. 1900, **C.**

784 Bird/Birdhouse, 4-1/8", Poland, c. 1900, **C.**

785 Horseman/Monument, 5-1/2", France, c. 1930, **E.**

786 Bird/Birdhouse, 4-7/8", Poland, c. 1930, **A.**

787 Elf With Bag, 3-3/4", German, c. 1880, **F.**

788 Boy/Empty Pockets, 4", German, c. 1900, **D.**

789 Elf On Ball, 5-5/8", German, c. 1870, **E.**

790 Hansel and Gretel, 2-5/8", German, c. 1885, **E.**

791 Knight/Horse, 6-3/4", France, c. 1930, **D.**

792 Bus, 2-1/4", German, c. 1930, **B.**

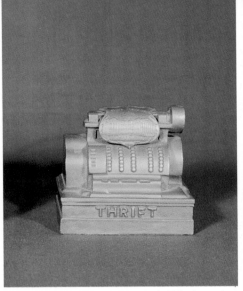

793 Cash Register, 2-3/8", American, c. 1935, **C.**

794 Key/Lock, 4", German, c. 1935, **D.**

795 Typewriter, 1-5/8", American, c. 1935, **C.**

796 Mantle Clock, 5-3/8", American, c. 1930, **D.**

797 Spanish Galleon, 3-3/4", German, c. 1920, **F.**

798 Mantle Clock, 4", American, c. 1930, **D.**

799 Apple, 2-1/2", Japan, c. 1920, **D.**

800 Soldier's Helmet, 3", German, c. 1920, **D.**

801 Walnut, 2-1/4", German, c. 1920, **C.**

802 Gate In Ulm Wall, 4-3/4", German, c. 1900, **C.**

803 Round Tower, 3-7/8", German, c. 1880, **D.**

804 Water Tower, 4-3/8", German, c. 1900, **D.**

805 Warsaw Town Hall, 3-5/8", Poland, c. 1900, **C.**

806 Hohenzollern Castle, 4", German, c. 1900, **C.**

807 Two Story House, 2-3/4", German, c. 1900, **C.**

808 Drachenfel Castle, 3-1/8", German, c. 1900, **C.**

809 Wilhelmshohe Castle, 4-1/4", German, c. 1900, **C.**

810 Windmill, 5-1/4", German, c. 1900, **D.**

811 Second Ward Savings Bank,
2-1/4", American, c. 1930, **C.**

812 Immanuel Lutheran Church,
6-1/2", American, c. 1938, **E.**

813 Dollar Savings Bank, 3-1/8",
American, c. 1930, **C.**

814 Loan & Trust Savings Bank,
2-1/2", American, c. 1930, **C.**

815 Neuschwenstein, 4-1/8",
German, c. 1900, **D.**

816 Knusperhauchen, 2-7/8",
German, c. 1930, **D.**

817 München Rathaus, 4-5/8",
German, c. 1930, **D.**

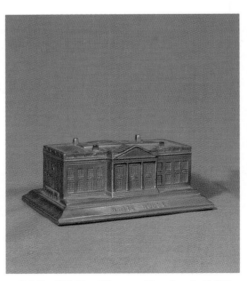

818 White House Bank, 1-5/8",
American, c. 1930, **C.**

819 Woolworth Building, 3-7/8",
American, c. 1930, **B.**

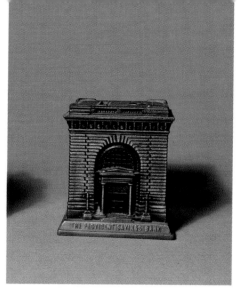

820 Provident Savings Bank,
3-1/2", American, c. 1930, **C.**

821 Empire State Building, 8",
Japan, c. 1950, **A.**

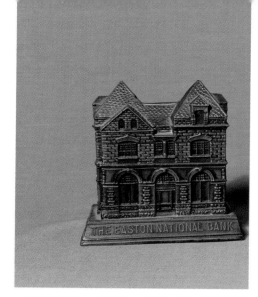

822 Eaton National Bank, 4-1/4",
American, c. 1930, **B.**

823 Jefferson Standard Life,
5-3/4", American, c. 1957, **A.**

824 Teepee, 4-3/8", American, c.
1939, **B.**

825 Tudor House, 3-1/4", American, c. 1920, **C.**

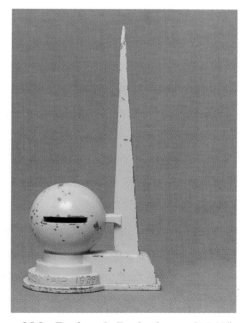

826 Trylon & Perisphere, 8-1/4",
American, c. 1939, **C.**

827 Riverside Bank, 5-1/2", American, c. 1930, **B.**

828 Trylon & Perisphere, 5-1/4",
American, c. 1939, **D.**

829 Gotham Bank Building, 6-3/8", American, c. 1918, **D.**

830 Cragin State Bank, 3-3/8", American, c. 1925, **D.**

831 WCTU Building, 4-5/8", American, c. 1891, **E.**

832 First National Bank, Davenport, 4", American, c. 1918, **D.**

833 Coast Federal Savings & Loan, 5-1/2", American, c. 1950, **C.**

834 Mission Dolores, S.F., 3-3/4", American, c. 1915, **D.**

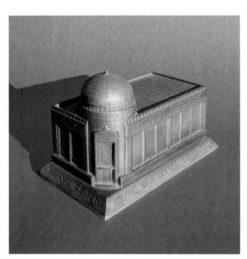

835 Miami Beach Federal Savings & Loan, 4", American, 1950, **C.**

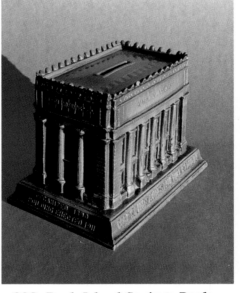

836 Rock Island Savings Bank, 3-1/2", American, c. 1911, **D.**

837 Corn Palace, 2-1/2", American, c. 1960, **B.**

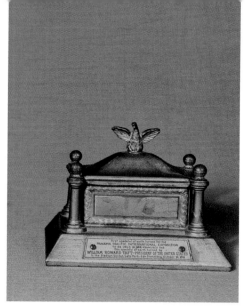

838 Panama Pacific Expo.,
3-1/4", American, c. 1915, **F.**

839 Eagle Knight Helmet, 5-1/2",
Japan, c. 1960, **A.**

840 Lion/Basket, 2-3/4", German,
c. 1900, **E.**

841 Birds In Nest, 3-3/8", German,
c. 1920, **E.**

842 Hot Air Balloon, 5", German,
c. 1880, **F.**

843 Pacific Coast Savings,
3-3/4", American, c. 1875, **D.**

844 Bank For Saving,
3", American, c. 1930, **B.**

845 Edison Phonograph, 3", American, c. 1930, **C.**

846 Bremen Rathaus Beehive,
3-1/4", German, c. 1920, **C.**

847 Washington Bust, 6", American, c. 1930, **C.**

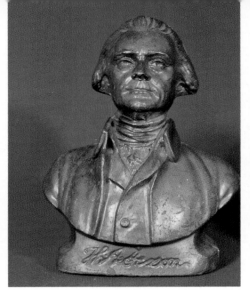

848 Jefferson Bust, 5-1/4", American, c. 1950, **A.**

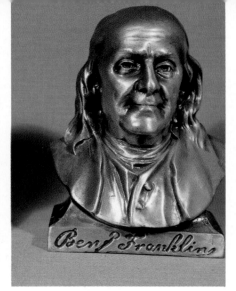

849 Ben Franklin Bust, 5-1/4", American, c. 1950, **A.**

850 La Salle Bust, 5-1/2", American, c. 1960, **A.**

851 Father Knickerbocker, 5", American, c. 1960, **B.**

852 Edison Bust, 6", American, c. 1950, **A.**

853 Chief Anacostia, 5-1/4", American, c. 1950, **B.**

854 'Annie' Costia, 5", American, c. 1950, **B.**

855 'Andy' Costia, 5-1/2", American, c. 1950, **B.**

856 Lincoln Bust, 5", American, c. 1920, **B.**

857 A. Lincoln, 5-1/8", American, c. 1950, **A.**

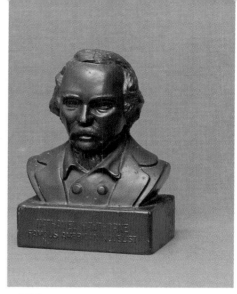

858 Hawthorne Bust, 5-1/4", American, c. 1950, **B.**

859 Horace Vernet Bust, 5-1/4", American, c. 1950, **B.**

860 Gobbo Bank, 4-1/2", American, c. 1909, **C.**

861 Roosevelt Bust, 6-1/4", American, c. 1930, **B.**

862 Notre Dame Bank, 6", American, c. 1950, **B.**

863 Purdue Bank, 6-3/4", American, c. 1950, **B.**

864 Buy Wise Owl, 6-1/2", American, c. 1950, **A.**

865 Globe, 3-7/8", American, c. 1930, **C.**

866 The General, 3-1/4", American, c. 1960, **B.**

867 Barrel, 3-3/8", American, c. 1950, **A.**

868 The Sportsman, 8-3/8" L., American, c. 1950, **B.**

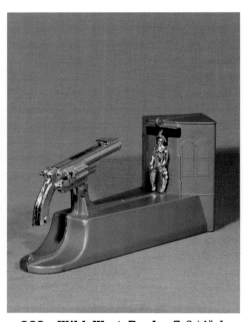

869 Wild West Bank, 7-3/4" L., American, c. 1950, **B.**

870 Southern Comfort, 8-1/2" L., American, c. 1950, **B.**

871 Rocket To Moon, 10-3/8", American, c. 1960, **B.**

872 Indian Head Penny, 3" dia., American, c. 1960, **A.**

873 Robot, 6", American, c. 1960, **A.**

CHAPTER 4

SILVER & BRASS

Silver, silver-plated and brass banks appear with some frequency in auctions and high-end antique shows. For many years European collectors have known the value of these banks created by fine artisans from the late 18th century well into the present century. Most of the specimens depicted here originated in Austria, Denmark, England, France and Germany. After 1875, American silversmiths began fashioning these treasures to satisfy the local needs for saving money.

Designers used a wide variety of alloys in producing their banks; pieces can be found fabricated from sterling silver (925/1000 silver), silver plating over nickel, brass, copper, or lead, and solid brass.

The majority of these banks are quite ornate and well crafted. They were fashioned in the shapes of animals, boxes, buildings, people, steins and urns. The steins and urns were usually engraved with a child's name and date of birth and ceremoniously presented to the family shortly after birth.

Often ornamentation took the form of stamped decoration. Bank pieces were soldered together. To retrieve the contents of the bank, designers created hinged lids with decorative hasps and small locks. A built-in key lock was an alternate method of keeping the bank secure. Many of the banks had raised coin slots with cloth, leather, rings or fingers that acted as guards to keep the coins from being shaken out. In some cases hinged key traps or screwed on bases were employed to gain access.

In 1875, Austrian bank makers fashioned decorative vermeil pieces often covered with faceted colorful crystals in the style of Malart. Many of the banks have identifying marks stamped into the base. One of the largest German manufacturers is WMF, Wurttembergische Metallwarenfabrick, founded in 1853 by Daniel Straub. Through several mergers, WMF grew to have several factories and 3,000 workers by 1950. Diversification has kept it an industry leader in our complex world. Ernst Dittmar of Nurnberg also made banks in the 1920s. Many brass banks were created as one of a kind designs by artisans who were commissioned to complete a bank for a particular occasion. These unique pieces stand alone in the fine collections found around the world.

Silver, silver-plated and brass banks must be carefully cleaned for they are subject to tarnish which greatly reduces their eye appeal. Never dip a bank in a liquid bath cleaner. Use only a polish that is mild and will not scratch the surface. It is important that the piece retain a classic patina. Dented pieces can be carefully repaired and silver plating re-applied, but it should be done only by professionals who know how to preserve the antique character of the bank.

One marvels at the intricacies of beautiful banks from another era when craftsmanship and art were merged into important elements of everyday life. They have survived the ravages of time to appear unscathed in today's world. It is no wonder that serious bank collectors search diligently in hopes of finding a wonderful piece.

874 Fluted Stein, 3-3/8", German, c. 1870, **F.**

875 Decorative Urn, 3", German, c. 1890, **E.**

876 Stein, 3-3/8", German, c. 1870, **F.**

877 Swirled Stein, 3-7/8", German, c. 1870, **F.**

878 Floral Urn, 4-1/2", German, c. 1870, **F.**

879 Stein/Head, 2-7/8", German, c. 1875, **E.**

880 Decorative Stein, 3-7/8", German, c. 1840, **F.**

881 3 Face Urn, 4-1/8", German, c. 1940, **F.**

882 Bird Urn, 4-1/8", German, c. 1875, **E.**

883 Beehive, 3-3/8", German, c. 1870, **E.**

884 Beer Barrel, 2-5/8", German, c. 1875, **E.**

885 Barrel, 2-7/8", England, c. 1900, **D.**

886 Canister, 4-1/4", German, c. 1900, **D.**

887 Bird, 2-1/2", German, c. 1875, **F.**

888 Urn, 3-7/8", German, c. 1880, **D.**

889 Faceted Stein, 2-1/2", German, c. 1870, **E.**

890 Art Deco Bank, 3", German, c. 1925, **F.**

891 Swirled Stein, 2-1/4", c. 1875, **E.**

892 Squirrel/Nut, 4-3/4", Denmark, c. 1930, **C.**

893 Brementown Barrel, 4-3/4", German, c. 1930, **D.**

894 Elephant, 3-5/8", Denmark, c. 1930, **E.**

895 Red Riding Hood, 2-5/8", German, c. 1900, **D.**

896 Rabbit, 2-1/4", Denmark, c. 1930, **D.**

897 Squirrel Box, 3", Denmark, c. 1930, **D.**

898 Statue of Liberty/Shell, 3", American, c. 1915, **D.**

899 Figural Barrel, 3", German, c. 1900, **E.**

900 Tree Canister, 3-1/4", Denmark, c. 1900, **E.**

901 Oriental House, 2-7/8", German, c. 1900, **E.**

902 Dog/Dog House, 2-1/2", American, c. 1930, **F.**

903 Hansel/Gretel. 3-3/4", Denmark, c. 1930, **C.**

904 Dog/Dog House, 2-5/8", German, c. 1859, **E.**

905 Tower, 6-1/4", Holland, c. 1875, **E.**

906 Dog/Dog House, 2-5/8", German, c. 1900, **E.**

907 Church/Two Chimneys, 3-7/8", German, c. 1880, **E.**

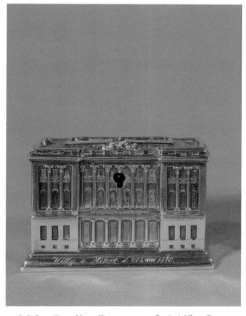

908 Berlin Bourse, 2-1/4", German, c. 1865, **F.**

909 Sparkasse, 2-3/8", German, c. 1865, **F.**

910 Windmill, 4-3/8", Holland, c. 1920, **D.**

911 Windmill, 5", Denmark, c. 1925, **C.**

912 Windmill, 5", Holland, c. 1900, **B.**

913 Chest, 2-1/8", German, c. 1900, **D.**

914 Decorative Carriage, 6", American, c. 1990, **F.**

915 Time To Save, 2-1/2", American, c. 1900, **E.**

916 Fish, 2-1/4", Unknown, c. 1930, **D.**

917 3 Dogs/Dog House, 2-3/4", American, c. 1920, **D.**

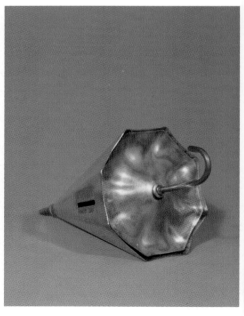

918 Umbrella, 2-3/4", American, c. 1930, **A.**

919 Stein, 3-1/2", Unknown, c. 1905, **D.**

920 Tapered Stein, 3-1/2", German, c. 1876, **C.**

921 Stein, 3-1/8", European, c. 1870, **D.**

922 Stein/Legs, 3-7/8", European, c. 1875, **D.**

923 Stein/Dog, 4-7/8", German, c. 1870, **F.**

924 Ringed Stein, 2-3/4", American, c. 1870, **C.**

925 Small Stein, 2-1/4", German, c. 1875, **C.**

926 Stein, 3-1/2", German, c. 1875, **D.**

927 Round Top Cup, 2-5/8", European, c. 1900, **C.**

928 Cup, 2-1/4", Unknown, c. 1935, **D.**

929 Vase, 3-3/4", European, c. 1890, **D.**

930 Oval Box, 3-1/8", England, c. 1890, **D.**

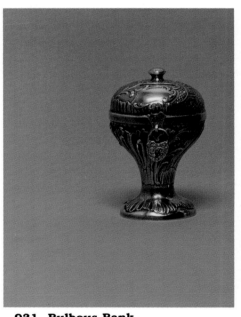

931 Bulbous Bank, 3-7/8", European, c. 1890, **F.**

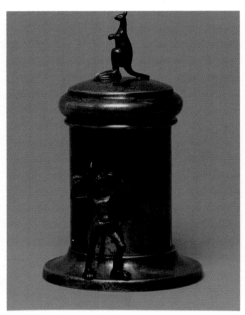

932 Kangaroo Bank, 6-5/8", Australian, c. 1920, **E.**

933 Flowered Bank, 4-1/4", Russian, c. 1880, **E.**

934 Animal Bank, 2-1/8", German, c. 1910, **D.**

935 Beeskept, 2-3/4", Norwegian, c. 1924, **C.**

936 Round Bank, 3", European, c. 1870, **D.**

937 Chest, 3-5/8", American, c. 1892, **F.**

938 Chest, 3-1/2", European, c. 1890, **E.**

939 Chest, 3-1/2", European, c. 1890, **E.**

940 Chest, 3-5/8", French, c. 1880, **F.**

941 Man/Umbrella, 5-1/4", American, c. 1900, **D.**

942 Dogs in Trunk, 2-1/2", German, c. 1915, **D.**

943 Jewish Pishce, 2-3/8", European, c. 1880, **E.**

944 Satchel Bank, 2-1/8", European, c. 1880, **C.**

945 Tapered Box, 1-7/8", German, c. 1910, **C.**

946 Beehive, 3-1/2", German, c. 1930, **B.**

947 Saltshaker Bank, 5", England, c. 1910, **D.**

948 Beehive, 3-3/8", Denmark, c. 1930, **C.**

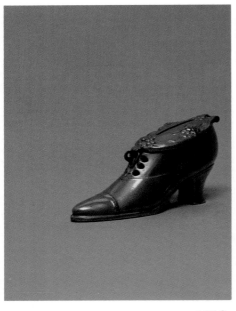

949 Shoe, 2-1/8", German, c. 1910, **D.**

950 Girl/Umbrella, 3-1/2", Denmark, c. 1935, **D.**

951 Dog/Barrel, 2-5/8", German, c. 1915, **D.**

952 Girl At Door, 4-1/2", German, c. 1910, **E.**

953 Bird/Base, 4", France, c. 1920, **E.**

954 Girls Head, 3", German, c. 1910, **D.**

955 Children/Drum, 2", American, c. 1925, **D.**

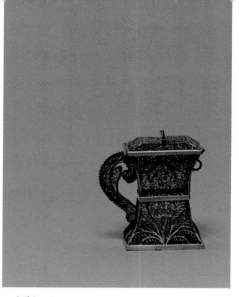

956 Fancy Pitcher, 2-5/8", European, c. 1870, **F.**

957 Drum, 2-3/8", American, c. 1930, **D.**

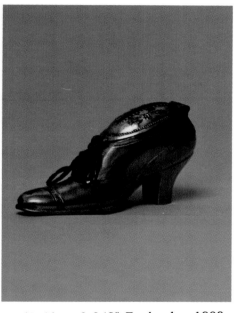

958 Shoe, 2-3/8", England, c. 1900, **D.**

959 Windmill, 4-1/8", German, c. 1930, **C.**

960 Deco Owl, 3-1/4", European, c. 1935, **E.**

961 Pocket Book, 3-1/8", European, c. 1900, **F.**

962 Dogs In Basket, 4-1/8", Japan, c. 1950, **B.**

963 Roll Top Desk, 3-5/8", German, c. 1900, **F.**

964 Stein, 4", German, c. 1850, **D.**

965 Stein, 4", German, c. 1850, **E.**

966 Floral Stein, 3-5/8", German, c. 1875, **F.**

967 Stein, 3-3/4", German, c. 1860, **E.**

968 Fluted Stein, 3-1/8", German, c. 1875, **F.**

969 Stein, 2-7/8", German, c. 1840, **F.**

970 Stein, 3", German, c. 1840, **E.**

971 Ringed Stein, 3", German, c. 1870, **F.**

972 Stein, 2-3/4", German, c. 1870, **D.**

973 Fluted Stein, 3-1/8", German, c. 1800, **E.**

974 Finger Handle Stein, 4", German, c. 1900, **D.**

975 Ornate Handle Stein, 3-1/2", German, c. 1875, **E.**

976 Decorative Stein, 3-3/8", German, c. 1880, **D.**

977 Decorative Stein, 3-1/8", German, c. 1880 , **E.**

978 Stein, 3-1/2", German, c. 1850, **D.**

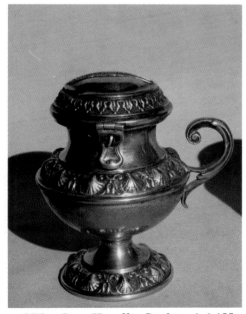

979 One Handle Stein, 4-1/8", France, c. 1875, **D.**

980 Round Top Stein, 3-3/4", German, c. 1880, **E.**

981 Decorative Urn, 3-7/8", France, c. 1875, **E.**

982 Pocketbook, 3-1/8", German, c. 1870, **E.**

983 Bell, 4", German, c. 1865, **D.**

984 Canister, 3-1/2", German, c. 1880, **E.**

985 Dog/Doghouse, 2-3/4", France, c. 1860, **D.**

986 Rabbit/Egg, 3-3/4", German, c. 1875, **F.**

987 Beehive, 3-1/2", Unknown, c. 1875, **E.**

988 Mushroom/Hive, 3", German, c. 1875, **D.**

989 Watering Can, 4-1/8", German, c. 1900, **D.**

990 Barrel On Legs, 3-3/4", German, c. 1900, **D.**

991 Pear, 3-1/2", Unknown, c. 1915, **D.**

992 Canister, 2-3/4", German, c. 1900, **D.**

993 Apple, 2-3/4", German, c. 1930, **C.**

994 Stein, 3", German, c. 1890, **C.**

995 Decorative Chest, 3-1/4", German, c. 1850, **F.**

996 Figure/Canister, 5", German, c. 1900, **D.**

997 Bureau, 2-1/2", German, c. 1870, **E.**

998 Chest, 2-3/8", Unknown, c. 1900, **D.**

999 Chest/Handle, 2-3/8", German, c. 1900, **E.**

1000 Windmill, 3-5/8", Unknown, c. 1900. **D.**

1001 Tower, 4-3/4", German, c. 1900, **D.**

1002 Windmill, 7-1/8", Unknown, c. 1900, **D.**

1003 Dog/Doghouse, 2-3/4", German, c. 1900, **E.**

1004 Stein/Figural Handle, 3-1/8", German, c. 1900, **E.**

1005 Elf/Mushroom, 4", German, c. 1875, **E.**

1006 Gazebo, 4-3/8", German, c. 1900, **D.**

1007 Guardhouse, 3", German, c. 1875, **F.**

1008 Swan/House, 3", France, c. 1900, **D.**

1009 Stein, 3-3/4", German, c. 1875, **D.**

Beehive, 3-1/8", German, c. 1890, **C.**

1011 Fluted Stein, 3-3/4", German, c. 1845, **F.**

1012 Jeweled Case, 2-1/8", Austrian, c. 1875, **E.**

1013 Birdhouse, 6-3/4", Austrian, c. 1875, **F.**

1014 Jeweled Case, 3-1/8", Austrian, c. 1875, **F.**

1016 Wheelbarrow, 4-1/4", Austrian, c. 1875, **E.**

1017 Goat Cart, 3-1/2", Austrian, c. 1875, **F.**

1015 Footed Chest, 3-1/4", Austrian, c. 1875, **E.**

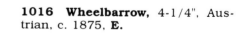
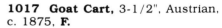

1018 Cross Shell, 6-1/2", German, c. 1915, **D.**

1019 Seaman Collection Box, 10", England, c. 1910, **E.**

1020 42cm Shell, 5", England, c. 1914, **F.**

1021 Pillar Bank, 6-1/4", England, c. 1930, **C.**

1022 Alarm Clock, 4-1/4", German, c. 1920, **F.**

1023 Vase, 7-1/2", France, c. 1850, **D.**

1024 Edward VII Crown, 3-3/4", England, c. 1905, **C.**

1025 Container, 3-3/8", German, c. 1870, **D.**

1026 Towel Rack, 6", England, c. 1910, **D.**

1027 Orleans Trust Co., 4-1/8", American, c. 1900, **D.**

1028 Golliwog, 6", England, c. 1915, **D.**

1029 Donald Duck, 6", Unknown, c. 1930, **C.**

1030 Bear Stealing Pig, 5", American, c. 1930, **C.**

1031 Rooster Pattern, 4-3/4", American, c. 1920, **E.**

1032 Eagle Savings Bank, 4-1/2", Israel, c. 1950, **C.**

1033 Bank Barrel, 3", England, c. 1900, **B.**

1034 Lantern, 3", German, c. 1920, **C.**

1035 Peepshow, 2-3/4", German, c. 1910, **F.**

1036 Bureaux Caisse/Eagle,
9-1/2", France, c. 1930, **F.**

1037 Vase Bank, 6-1/2", Unknown,
c. 1930, **D.**

1038 Caisse Bank/Bird,
7-3/4", France, c. 1930, **E.**

1039 Crown/Ball, 6-1/4", Sweden,
c. 1900, **D.**

1040 Bench, 4-1/2 ", American, c.
1914, **E.**

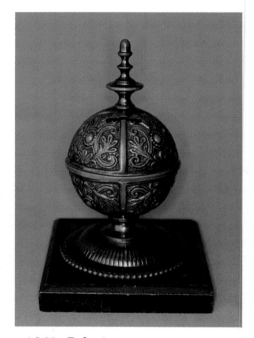

1041 Balustervase,
8", Germany, c. 1830, **E.**

1042 Trunk, 2", Russian, c. 1900,
E.

1043 Lindbergh Plane, 5-1/4",
American, c. 1925, **D.**

1044 House With Chimney,
3-1/2", Russian, c. 1900, **E.**

1045 Building/Soldier, 7-1/4", France, c. 1900, **D.**

1046 Caisse/Bird, 4-1/4", France, c. 1900, **C.**

1047 Caisse Bank, 4-3/4", France, c. 1900, **C.**

1048 Den Danske Landmandsbank, 4-1/2", Denmark, c. 1904, **B.**

1049 Covenant Presbyterian, 2-3/8", American Pattern, c. 1930, **E.**

1050 Bureaux Caisse, 9-1/2", France, c. 1890, **D.**

1051 Birth Bank, 7-1/2", England, c. 1880, **E.**

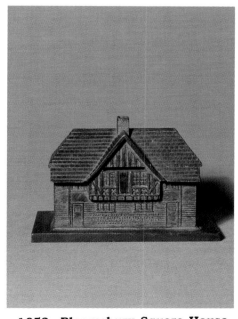

1052 Bloomsbury Square House, 4", England c. 1920, **D.**

1053 Windmill, 6", German, c. 1930, **C.**

CHAPTER 5

TIN, REGISTERS AND POCKETS

The process for making tin plate originated in Germany during the 15th century. By 1720, tin plate manufacturing was well established in England. Fifty years later, the first tinware factory in America was established in Berlin, Connecticut. We know that colonial peddlers carried lightweight tin money boxes on their travels throughout America. During the first half of the 19th century, tinsmiths fabricated banks by hand, using punching, rolling and crimping tools to bend and solder the raw metal and create simple money boxes. George Brown designed a line of tin banks in the 1850s. His merger with the J. & E. Stevens company of Cromwell, Connecticut, in 1870, led to the development of a full line of architectural tin cottages and steeple churches that were painted and stenciled. Weeden produced a series of tin windup banks in the 1880s. In 1903, J. Chein and Co., of New York, produced a number of brightly colored lithographed tin toys. The earliest Chein banks were the *Child's Fireproof* and *Mascot Safes* produced around 1905. Chein manufactured a large inventory of tin banks until the 1970s. Other American tin bank makers include Bankers Advertising Co., Buddy "L" Co., John Hugo Mfg. Co., Louis Marx & Co. and Ferdinand Strauss Corp. In Europe, tin bank demands were filled by great companies like Lehmann, Marklin and Selheimer & Strauss in Germany and Burnett Limited in England. Today, tin bank orders are filled by companies in Japan, China and Russia.

Register Banks

Beginning in 1929, pocket dime registering banks were made, depicting a wide variety of subjects. Many of the more popular banks show cartoon characters and heroes of the period. During the 1940s, a series of patriotic banks emerged featuring airplanes, battleships and tanks. These banks collected coins to be used in the war efforts. Not to be outdone, companies including Coca-Cola and General Electric used the small banks as effective means of advertising their products. Finally, there was a series of nickel plated banks featuring important landmarks in the United States, such as the Capitol Building, Empire State Building, and the Statue of Liberty. Most of the banks are 2-1/2" square and were manufactured by Kalon Mfg. Co. and Chein from 1929 to 1964. Originally the banks sold for 29 cents each. Today, collectors pay high prices for a few of the rare specimens.

Pocket Banks

Small enough to be kept in the pocket, these banks were ready receptacles to save coins for a rainy day. There are many types: celluloid advertising banks, nickel plated watches and horseshoes, banks that fit into pencil boxes, and prizes in Cracker Jacks. Book banks, usually made by Zell Products, were manufactured in great numbers and distributed by banking institutions.

There are hundreds of small satchel banks that were created to keep your savings. Many were nickel, chrome, and electroplated with small die-stamped advertising plates firmly affixed to the bank. Banking personnel retained the key so the owner had to bring the coin bank back to get the coins out and presumably deposited into a savings account. A small sampling of these banks is contained here; so many varieties exist that an entire book could be filled with them alone.

1054 Bearded Man, 3-3/4", German, c. 1930, **D.**

1055 Woman/Clasped Hands, 3-3/4", German, c. 1930, **D.**

1056 Sailor, 5", American, c. 1930, **D.**

1057 Humpty Dumpty, 5", American, c. 1930, **D.**

1058 Round Soldier, 2-1/2", German, c. 1930, **E.**

1059 Round Clown, 2-1/2", German, c. 1930, **E.**

1060 Poor Weary Willie, 4-3/4", England, c. 1930, **D.**

1061 Money Saved Here, 5-3/4", American, c. 1930, **E.**

1062 Poor Tired Tim, 4-3/4", England, c. 1930, **D.**

1063 Roly Poly Monkey, 6", American, c. 1930, **D.**

1064 Man/Cap & Bowtie, 2-1/4", American, c. 1930, **D.**

1065 Humpty Dumpty, 6", American, c. 1935, **C.**

1066 Mickey/Post Office, 4-3/4", England, c. 1950, **C.**

1067 Oval Santa Bank, 3", American, c. 1930, **C.**

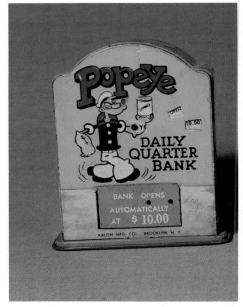

1068 Popeye Daily Quarter Bank, 4-3/4", American, c. 1950, **D.**

1069 Army Man, 4", Japan, c. 1960, **B.**

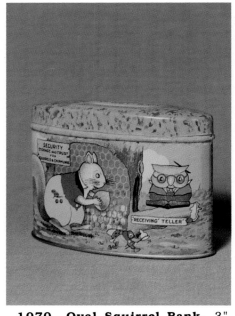

1070 Oval Squirrel Bank, 3", American, c. 1930, **C.**

1071 Old King Cole Bank, 3-7/8" American, c. 1930, **C.**

1072 Dodge Barrel, 3-3/4", American, c. 1930, **C.**

1073 Camel Bank, 3", American, c. 1930, **B.**

1074 Dodge Drum, 3-1/4", American, c. 1930, **C.**

1075 Bab-O Bank, 3", American, c. 1925, **C.**

1076 Babbitts Cleanser, 5", American, c. 1920, **C.**

1077 Old Dutch Cleanser, 3", American, c. 1925, **C.**

1078 Thermo Bank, 2-3/4", American, c. 1940, **A.**

1079 Libby's Treasure, 3-1/2", American, c. 1939, **A.**

1080 Sapolin Bank, 1-7/8", American, c. 1925, **C.**

1081 Medical Donation Bank, 6-3/8", England, c. 1925, **E.**

1082 Federal Washing Machine, 4-1/4", American, c. 1920, **C.**

1083 Century Of Progress, 3-1/2", American, c. 1939, **A.**

1084 Twinkle Bank, 2", American, c. 1930, **D.**

1085 Universal Stoves, 3-7/8", American, c. 1890, **E.**

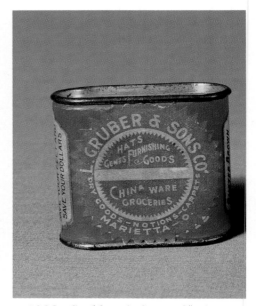

1086 Grubber & Sons, 2", American, c. 1930, **D.**

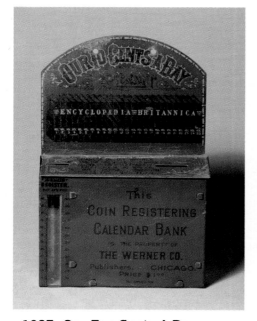

1087 Our Ten Cents A Day, 7-3/4", American, c. 1900, **E.**

1088 Uncle Don Bank, 2-1/4", American, c. 1940, **C.**

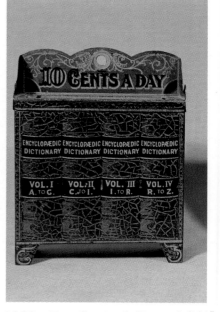

1089 Ten Cents A Day, 4-3/4", American, c. 1898, **E.**

1090   Dick Whittington/Cat, 5",
England, c. 1920, **C.**

1091   Queen Alexander/King Edward VII, 2-1/2", England, c. 1900,
C.

1092   Pillar Box, 5", Holland, c.
1929, **B.**

1093   Tin Stein, 3-3/4", German,
c. 1845, **E.**

1094   Three Dial Safe, 5-1/8", German, c. 1950, **B.**

1095   Early Stein, 2-1/2", German,
c. 1840, **F.**

1096   S. Olaf Bank,
5", Holland, c. 1922, **C.**

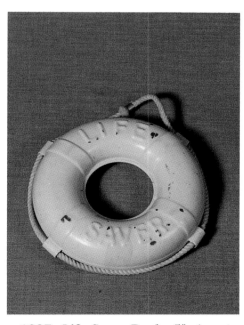

1097   Life Saver Bank, 5", American, c. 1930, **D.**

1098   West Berlin Bank, 2-1/4",
German, c. 1950, **A.**

1099 Punch & Judy, 2-3/4", German, c. 1900, **D.**

1100 Hansel & Gretel, 2-1/8", German, c. 1900, **D.**

1101 Chalet Bank, 1-7/8", German, c. 1920, **C.**

1102 Two Story Savings Bank, 5-3/4", American, c. 1850, **D.**

1103 Bank Building, 4", American, c. 1860, **D.**

1104 Bank Building, 4", American, c. 1860, **D.**

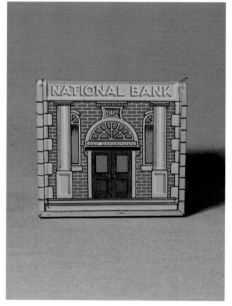

1105 National Bank, 3", American, c. 1940, **B.**

1106 Bank Building, 4-3/8", American, c. 1870, **C.**

1107 House In Snow, 3-1/2", American, c. 1940, **B.**

1108 Roll Top Desk, 4-1/4", American, c. 1875, **F.**

1109 Sewing Machine, 5", American, c. 1900, **E.**

1110 Oriental Table, 3-1/4", American, c. 1930, **C.**

1111 Li'l Abner, 4-1/2", American, c. 1950, **B.**

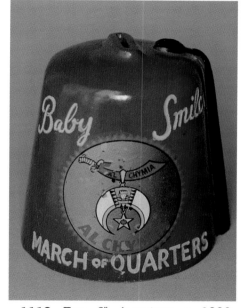

1112 Fez, 6", American, c. 1930, **C.**

1113 Chad Valley, 5-3/4", England. c. 1930, **B.**

1114 Radio Bank, 4-3/4", American, c. 1950, **C.**

1115 Television Bank, 5-1/2", American, c. 1950, **C.**

1116 Radio Bank, 4-1/4", American, c. 1950, **C.**

1117 Watering Can, 4", German, c. 1908, **C.**

1118 Noah's Ark, 3-1/2", Israel, c. 1953, **D.**

1119 Alarm Clock, 3", American, c. 1930, **C.**

1120 Your Weight Scale, 6-1/2", American, c. 1930, **D.**

1121 Jitney, 4-1/2", American, c. 1930, **F.**

1122 Guess Your Weight, 5-1/4", American, c. 1930, **D.**

1123 Children's Stein, 3-1/4", German, c. 1930, **C.**

1124 American Fence, 4-1/2", American, c. 1930, **B.**

1125 Windmill, 4", Holland, c. 1930, **B.**

1126 Super Market, 2-3/4", American, c. 1950, **B.**

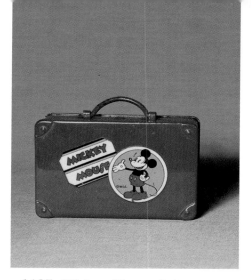

1127 Mickey Mouse Suitcase, 2-1/2", American, c. 1935, **E.**

1128 Paying Teller, 3-1/4", German, c. 1950, **A.**

1129 Mouse House, 3-1/2", Japan, c. 1950, **B.**

1130 Clock Bank, 3", American, c. 1950, **B.**

1131 Church Bank, 3-1/4", Japan, c. 1950, **B.**

1132 Buick Fireball, 4-1/2", American, c. 1949, **B.**

1133 Patton's Sunproof Paint, 2", American, c. 1930, **B.**

1134 Chevrolet Globe, 4-1/2", American, c. 1940, **C.**

1135 Thrift Bank, 4", American, c. 1930, **C.**

1136 Get Rich Quick, 3-1/2", American, c. 1940, **C.**

1137 Thrift Bank, 4", American, c. 1925, **D.**

1138 Donald Duck Bank, 4", American, c. 1940, **E.**

1139 Federal Reg. Dime Bank, 4-3/4", American, c. 1920, **D.**

1140 Lincoln Quarter Reg. 3-1/4", American, c. 1950, **C.**

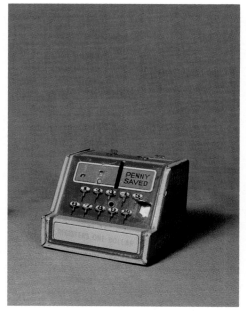

1141 Walgreen Penny Saver, 2-1/4", American, c. 1950, **C.**

1142 U Save A Dime, 3-3/4", American, c. 1950, **C.**

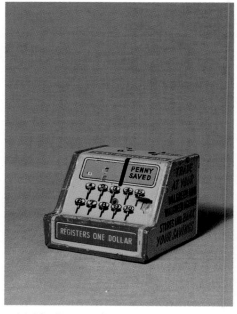

1143 Penny Saver, 2-1/4", American, c. 1950, **A.**

1144 Baseball Bank, 4-1/2", American, c. 1940, **D.**

1145 Scenic Box, 2-1/4", German, c. 1930, **C.**

1146 Roy Rogers Savings, 8", American, c. 1950, **B.**

1147 Band Playing Bank, 3-1/4", Canada, c. 1950, **B.**

1148 Children Registering, 4-3/4", German, c. 1950, **C.**

1149 Texas Ranger Savings, 8", American, c. 1950, **B.**

1150 Kittens Bank, 6", England, c. 1950, **B.**

1151 Log Cutting Bank, 6-3/4", American, c. 1950, **C.**

1152 Dog Bank, 6", England, c. 1950, **B.**

1153 Saving Bank,
4-3/4", Japan, c. 1930, **B.**

1154 Keyless Savings,
5-1/4", American, c. 1890, **F.**

1155 Broadway Savings Bank,
3-3/4", American, c. 1930, **C.**

1156 Green Safe, 4-7/8", German,
c. 1930, **B.**

1157 Vault Bank/3 Dial, 3-3/4",
American, c. 1930, **B.**

1158 Safe Bank, 3-7/8", American,
c. 1920, **A.**

1159 Home Savings Bank, 4-1/8",
England, c. 1930, **B.**

1160 National Bank, 5-5/8", Unknown, c. 1950, **A.**

1161 My Secret Safe, 4-7/8", Germany, c. 1930, **B.**

1162 Mascot Safe, 4", American, c. 1915, **D.**

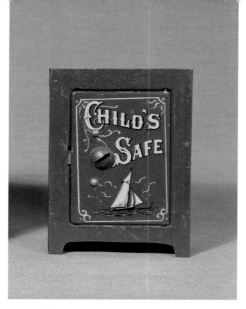

1163 Child's Safe, 3-7/8", American, c. 1915, **D.**

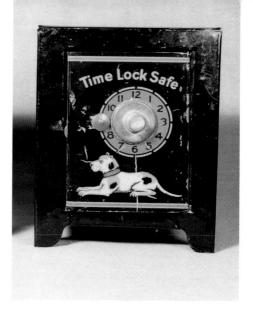

1164 Time Lock Safe, 5-1/2", American, c. 1930, **C.**

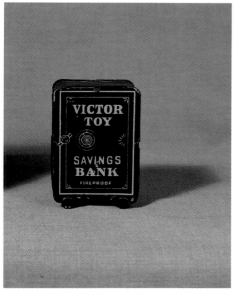

1165 Victor Toy Savings, 2-5/8", American, c. 1930, **D.**

1166 Sun Dial Bank, 4-3/8", American, c. 1930, **C.**

1167 Filitup Savings Bank, 3-7/8", American, c. 1930, **D.**

1168 Child's Safe, 2-3/4", American, c. 1915, **D.**

1169 Child's Safe, 2-5/8", American, c. 1930, **C.**

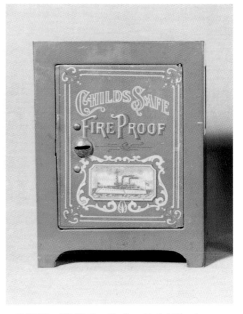

1170 Child's Safe, 5-1/2", American, c. 1930, **D.**

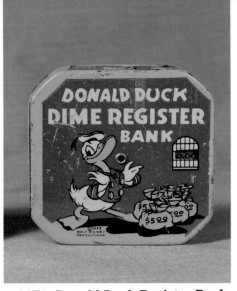

1171 Donald Duck Register Bank, 2-1/2", American, c. 1939, **E.**

1172 Mickey Mouse Register Bank, 2-1/2", American, c. 1939, **E.**

1173 Snow White Register Bank, 2-1/2", American, c. 1938, **B.**

1174 Popeye Daily Dime Bank, 2-1/2", American, c. 1956, **B.**

1175 Superman Dime Register Bank, 2-1/2", American, c. 1940, **D.**

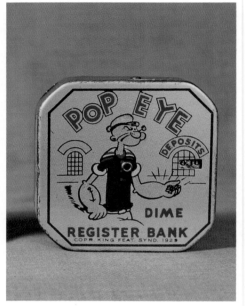

1176 Popeye Dime Register Bank, 2-1/2", American, c. 1929, **A.**

1177 Davy Crockett Dime Bank, 2-1/2", American, c. 1950, **D.**

1178 Capt. Marvel Magic Dime Saver, 2-1/2", American, c. 1948, **D.**

1179 Prince Valiant Dime Bank, 2-1/2", American, c. 1954, **D.**

1180 Astronaut Daily Dime Bank,
2-1/2", American, c. 1950, **A.**

1181 Clown & Monkey Bank,
2-1/2", American, c. 1956, **A.**

1182 Jackie Robinson Reg. Bank,
2-1/2", American, c. 1947, **E.**

1183 Cowboy Daily Dime Bank,
2-1/2", American, c. 1949, **A.**

1184 Daily Dime Piggy Bank,
2-1/2", American, c. 1949, **A.**

1185 Vacation Daily Dime Bank,
2-1/2", American, c. 1949, **A.**

1186 Thrifty Dime Reg. Bank,
2-1/2", American, c. 1945, **C.**

1187 Mercury Dime Reg. Bank,
2-1/2", American, c. 1945, **C.**

1188 Uncle Sam Dime Reg. Bank,
2-1/2", American, c. 1942, **D.**

TIN, REGISTERS, AND POCKETS   145

1189 "Keep 'Em Smiling" Reg. Bank, 2-1/2", American, c. 1942, **D.**

1190 "Keep 'Em Sailing" Reg. Bank, 2-1/2", American, c. 1942, **D.**

1191 "Keep 'Em Rolling" Reg. Bank, 2-1/2", American, c. 1942, **D.**

1192 Dopey Dime Register Bank, 2-1/2", American, c. 1939, **E.**

1193 "Keep 'Em Flying" Reg. Bank, 2-1/2", American, c. 1945, **D.**

1194 Little Orphan Annie Reg. Bank, 2-1/2", American, c. 1936, **D.**

1195 Elf Dime Register Bank, 2-1/2", American, c. 1937, **C.**

1196 New York World's Fair Bank, 2-1/2", American, c. 1964, **B.**

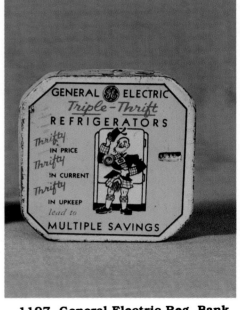

1197 General Electric Reg. Bank, 2-1/2", American, c. 1937, **D.**

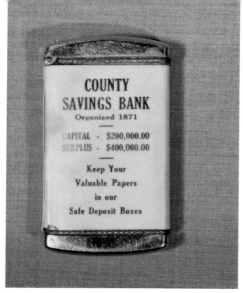

1198 County Savings Bank,
2-5/8", American, c. 1930, **D.**

1199 Savings Dime Bank,
2-5/8", American, c. 1930, **D.**

1200 Old South Trust Co., 2-5/8",
American c. 1930, **D.**

1201 The Union Bank, 3-1/2",
American, c. 1930, **C.**

1202 Dime Bank, 2-1/2", American, c. 1930, **C.**

1203 Miami Valley National Bank,
3-3/8", American, c. 1930, **D.**

1204 Dollar Dime Saver, 4", American, c. 1930, **C.**

1205 Olean National Bank Watch,
2-3/4", American, c. 1915, **F.**

1206 Eberhard Faber Watch,
2-3/4", American, c. 1925, **E.**

1207 Thrift Bank,
1-5/8", American, c. 1930, **C.**

1208 Saving Bank,
1-5/8", American, c. 1930, **C.**

1209 Harold Lloyd Bank, 2-1/4",
American, c. 1930, **E.**

1210 Penny Bank, 1-1/2", American, c. 1930, **B.**

1211 Red Goose Penny Bank,
1-5/8", American, c. 1930, **C.**

1212 Thrift Bank,
1-5/8", American, c. 1930, **B.**

1213 American Lead Pencil Co.,
1-5/8", American, c. 1930, **C.**

1214 Indian/Saving Bank, 1-5/8",
American, c. 1930, **C.**

1215 Airplane/Coin Bank,
1-5/8", American, c. 1930, **C.**

1216 VOW Bank, 2-1/2", American, c. 1918, **E.**

1217 Stag Shirts, 2", American, c. 1925, **E.**

1218 One Dime Saved Me, 2", American, c. 1925, **D.**

1219 County Savings Bank, 2-1/2", American, c. 1920, **D.**

1220 Klan Haven, 2", American, c. 1920, **E.**

1221 Glory To God Bank, 2", American, c. 1930, **C.**

1222 Roosevelt Savings Bank, 2-1/2", American, c. 1920, **D.**

1223 Special Aids Society, 2", American, c. 1920, **D.**

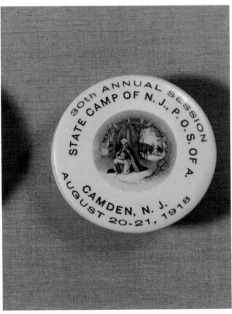

1224 State Camp Bank, 2", American, c. 1920, **D.**

1225 Eagle Pencil Thrift Bank,
1-7/8", American, c. 1930, **C.**

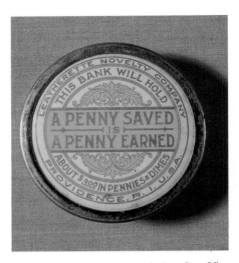

1226 A Penny Saved Bank, 2",
American, c. 1920, **C.**

1227 Goody Bank, 2", American,
c. 1930, **C.**

1228 Fireman Bank,
2", American, c. 1915, **F.**

1229 Buffalo Sled Co., Front, 2-
1/2", American, c. 1920, **F.**

1230 Buffalo Sled Co., Back,
2-1/2", American, c. 1920, **F.**

**1231 B.F.B. Permanent Blind
Relief,** 2", American, c. 1918, **C.**

1232 Save Your Pennies, 2", American, c. 1925, **C.**

1233 Widows And Orphans, 2",
American, c. 1920, **D.**

1234 One Dime Saved Me, 2-1/2", American, c. 1925, **B.**

1235 Ladies Auxiliary, 2-1/2", American, c. 1925, **B.**

1236 Starr Commonwealth For Boys, 2", American, c. 1930, **C.**

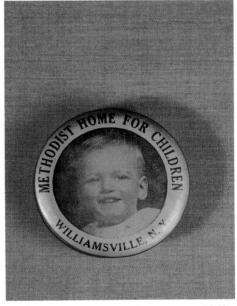

1237 Methodist Home For Children, 2", American, c. 1930, **C.**

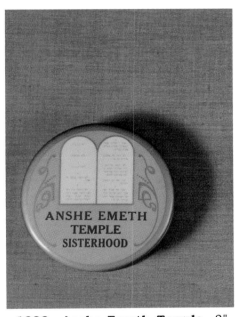

1238 Anshe Emeth Temple, 2", American, c. 1923, **C.**

1239 Klan Haven, N.Y., 2", American, c. 1923, **C.**

1240 Merchant and Illinois National Bank, 3-1/2", American, c. 1920, **C.**

1241 Savings Bank of Utica, 3-1/2", American, c. 1920, **D.**

1242 Farmer's and Merchant Bank, 3-1/2", American, c. 1920, **B.**

1243 Luthers Bank, 2", American, c. 1920, **C.**

1244 Flag Bank, 2-1/2", American, c. 1930, **C.**

1245 Belgian Soldier's Tobacco Fund, 2", American, c. 1920, **C.**

1246 The Pennsylvania Trust Co., 2-3/4", American, c. 1920, **C.**

1247 American Trust & Savings Bank, 2-1/2", American, c. 1925, **C.**

1248 Woodstock Children's Home, 2-3/4", American, c. 1920, **B.**

1249 Maumkeag Trust Co., 2-1/2", American, c. 1926, **C.**

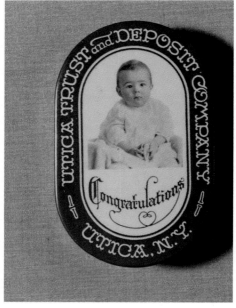

1250 Utica Trust & Deposit, 3-1/4", American, c. 1920, **D.**

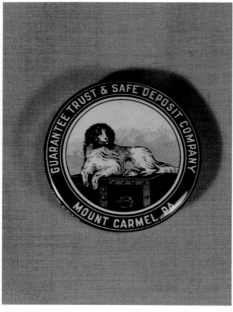

1251 Guarantee Trust, 2-1/2", American, c. 1925, **C.**

1252 Fidelity Trust Co., 3-1/4", American, c. 1925, **C.**

1253 Monroe County Savings, 2-1/2", American, c. 1930, **D.**

1254 Alarm Clock Bank, 2-1/4", American, c. 1930, **D.**

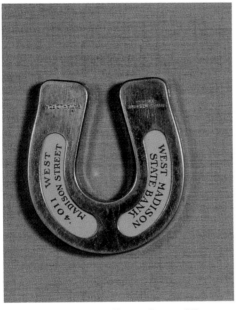

1255 West Madison State/Horseshoe, 3", American, c. 1930, **D.**

1256 Good Luck Bank, 1", American, c. 1930, **C.**

1257 Horseshoe Bank, 2-3/4", American, c. 1930, **D.**

1258 Clock Bank, 1-7/8", American, c. 1930, **C.**

1259 Saving Bank, 3-1/4", American, c. 1930, **B.**

1260 Clock Bank, 1-7/8", American, c. 1930, **D.**

1261 Wells Fargo Bank, 4-1/2",
American, c. 1945, **C.**

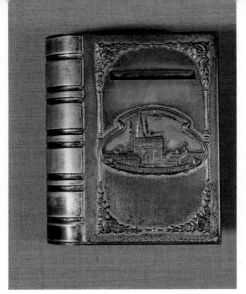

1262 Munster in Strassburg Bank,
3-1/2", German, c. 1930, **C.**

1263 N.Y. World's Fair, 4-1/2",
American, c. 1939, **E.**

1264 Mickey Mouse, 4-1/4",
American, c. 1939, **E.**

1265 V For Victory,
4-1/4", American, c. 1942, **D.**

1266 Scrappy Bank,
3-1/2", American, c. 1930, **D.**

1267 Mother Lode Bank, 4-1/2",
American, c. 1940, **C.**

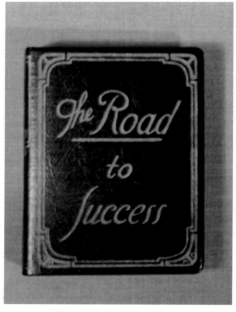

1268 Road To Success,
3", American, c. 1930, **C.**

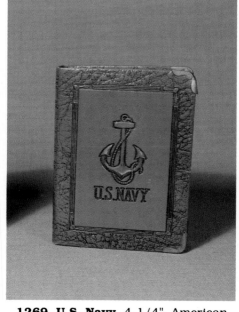

1269 U.S. Navy, 4-1/4", American,
c. 1940, **C.**

1270 The Roosevelt Bank, 4-1/4", American, c. 1940, **B.**

1271 Washington Mutual, 2-1/2", American, c. 1920, **B.**

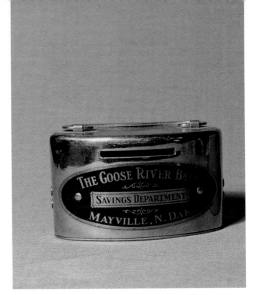

1272 Goose River Bank, 2", American, c. 1928, **B.**

1273 Toledo Scale Co., 2", American, c. 1930, **B.**

1274 Dutch Satchel, 2-1/2", Holland, c. 1950, **A.**

1275 Midtown Savings Clock, 3-1/4", American, c. 1930, **C.**

1276 Satchel, 3-1/4", American, c. 1910, **C.**

1277 SBCCA Book Bank, 3-1/2", American, c. 1986, **C.**

1278 SBCCA Rocking Horse Bank, 4-3/8", American, c. 1994, **C.**

CHAPTER 6
WOOD, GLASS & PAPER

Wooden Banks

Wooden banks have been with us for a long time. The first ones were collection boxes used by religious orders or socially conscious organizations to provide money for worthy causes. Mauchline Ware wooden banks were made from sycamore wood and usually decorated with transfer prints. They were made in Mauchline, Scotland, from the early 19th century until the factory burned in 1933. Other wooden banks from this era include Tunbridge Ware, Tartan Ware, and Black Lacquer Ware. These wooden banks were exported to countries all over the world.

In the 1920s and '30s, Tramp Art banks entered the market having been made from hand carved wood salvaged from cigar boxes. Coinciding with their appearance were Japanese inlaid trick banks that were exported to America. Since wood was scarce in Japan, a process of inlay called "yuseki" was employed to produce thin slices of differently colored woods used to inlay. Boxes and buildings were the favorite subject matter for these bank artists. Great care was taken to conceal slots, locks, and traps, assuring the owner that the coins saved would be secure. Many other types of wooden banks were made during the 20th century. From 1930-1950, large numbers of wooden banks were created from logs and were sold in local tourist attractions.

Glass Banks

The earliest American glass banks were made in the shape of hand-blown balls. Deming Jarves, of the Boston and Sandwich Glass Works in Massachusetts, created a very ornate, 18" tall, decorated glass bank in the 1830s for one of the glass blower's daughters. By the turn of the century, glass factories began producing convertible slotted cap banks commercially for the food industry. Candy companies began packaging their products in pressed glass banks in the 1920s and continued to the 1950s.

Paper Banks

There was an explosion of paper banks when color lithography was first employed as a means of advertising a company or product. Early paper banks are found in the forms of savings envelopes or boxes. Much later, folded paper dime savers appeared. Due to a shortage of materials, paper banks were used to raise money during both World Wars to buy Thrifty's and War Bonds. Once again, the food industry cashed in on inexpensive ways to advertise their products, especially small dairies.

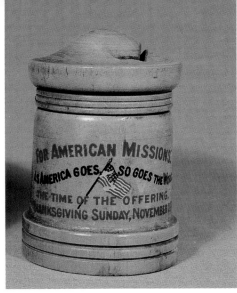

1279 American Missions Bank,
4", England, c. 1915, **D.**

1280 New Chelsea Bridge Bank,
3-1/2", England, c. 1860, **E.**

1281 Battleship Oregon Bank,
3-7/8", England, c. 1915, **D.**

1282 Teapot Bank, 3-5/8", England, c. 1875, **D.**

1283 Turned Wood Bank, 2", England, c. 1880, **E.**

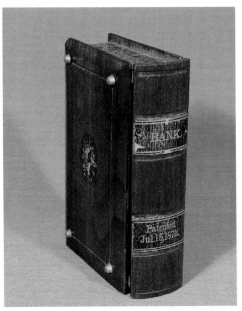

1284 Bank Book, 5-1/4", American, c. 1875, **E.**

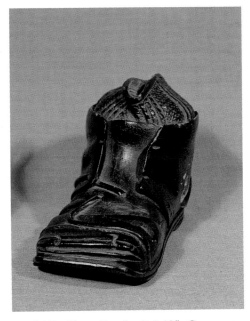

1285 Shoe Bank, 3-1/2", German, c. 1920, **D.**

1286 Tramp Art Bank, American, 4-3/4", c. 1920, **F.**

1287 Money Box, 4-3/8" w. German, c. 1930, **B.**

1288 House, 4", Japan, c. 1930, **B.**

1289 Bird House, 3-1/8", Japan, c. 1950, **B.**

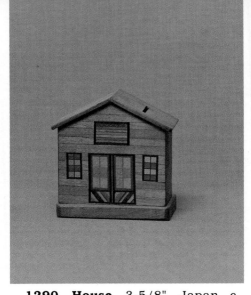

1290 House, 3-5/8", Japan, c. 1940, **B.**

1291 Two Story Building, 3-1/2", Japan, c. 1935, **C.**

1292 Mill Bank, 6", Japan, c. 1950, **D.**

1293 Building, 4-3/8", Japan, c. 1935, **C.**

1294 Scotties, 3-1/8", Japan, c. 1935, **C.**

1295 Two Story House, 5-5/8", Japan, c. 1935, **C.**

1296 Layered Box, 2-1/4", Japan, c. 1935, **B.**

1297 Carved Face, 3-1/2", Central America, c. 1895, **E.**

1298 Matruska Doll, 6", Russian, c. 1930, **C.**

1299 Black Face, 3-7/8", American, c. 1890, **D.**

1300 Decorative Jar, 4", German, c. 1890, **D.**

1301 Furnace/Mt. Fuji, 6", Japan, c. 1930, **C.**

1302 Slave Collection Box, 2-3/4", England, c. 1885, **D.**

1303 Missions To Seaman, 4-1/2", England, c. 1910, **D.**

1304 Brownie Book, 6", Scotland, c. 1920, **E.**

1305 Rooster On Basket, 5-1/2", German, c. 1929, **D.**

1306 New York World's Fair, 3-1/4", American, c. 1939, **B.**

1307 New York World's Fair, 3" dia., American, c. 1939, **C.**

1308 Savings Bank, 4", American, c. 1930, **C.**

1309 Charlie Chaplin, 3-3/4", American, c. 1920, **D.**

1310 Save With Major. 2-1/4", England, c. 1940, **C.**

1311 Kewpie, 3-1/4", American, c. 1919, **D.**

1312 Glass Safe Bank, 3-1/2", American, c. 1935, **B.**

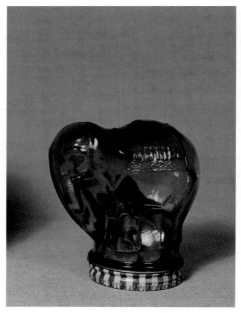

1313 Jumbo Peanut Elephant, 3-1/2", American, c. 1930, **D.**

1314 Savings Bank, 3-7/8", American, c. 1930, **C.**

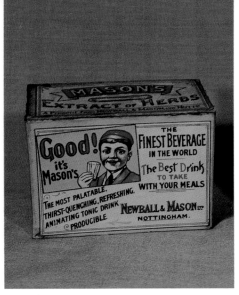

1315 Mason's Penny Bank,
3-1/8", England, c. 1880, **F.**

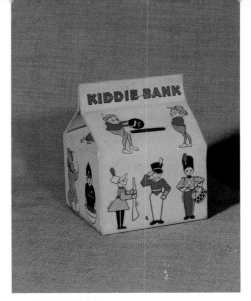

1316 Kiddie Bank, 3-1/2", American, c. 1983, **C.**

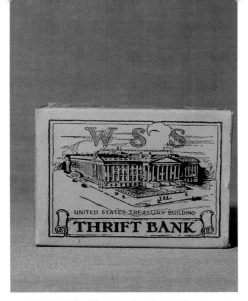

1317 Thrift Bank, 2-1/2", American, c. 1914, **E.**

1318 Cornucopia Bank,
5-5/8", American, c. 1885, **F.**

1319 Every Dime Counts, 4-1/2", American, c. 1918, **E.**

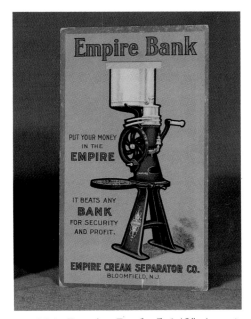

1320 Empire Bank, 5-1/2", American, c. 1880, **F.**

1321 Peoples Savings Bank,
4-1/4", American, c. 1935, **D.**

1322 Home Savings Bank, 5-3/4", American c. 1930, **D.**

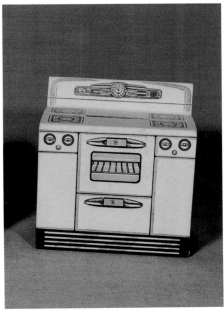

1323 Tappan Range Bank, 3-3/4", American, c. 1949, **C.**

WOOD, GLASS & PAPER 161

CHAPTER 7

NEW FINDS

It takes several years to write a book on penny banks. Late additions are necessary if we are to grow with our hobby and not become static. The following group illustrates some newer banks depicting a number of heroes and cartoon characters of our era, as well as some great new finds from collectors who continue to search every corner of the penny bank market. There are many penny banks yet to be uncovered in some obscure flea market or antiques store.

1324 SBCCA Soldier Bank,
7-1/2", American, c. 1982, **C.**

1325 SBCCA Florida Bank,
5-1/4", American, c. 1988, **C.**

1326 SBCCA St. Louis Arch,
4-1/4", American, c. 1987, **C.**

1327 Santa Claus, 7", American, c. 1930, **C.**

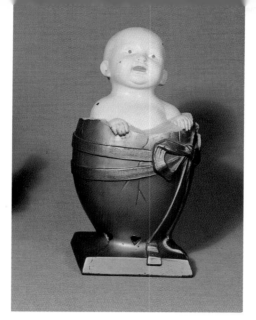

1328 Baby/Egg, 7-1/2", American, c. 1924, **E.**

1329 Expo 86 Bank, 5-5/8", China, c. 1986, **B.**

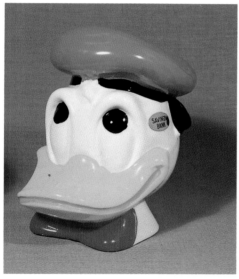

1330 Donald Duck, 5-3/8", Japan, c. 1960, **B.**

1331 Howdy Doody, 4-1/2", Japan, c. 1970, **C.**

1332 Li'l Orphan Annie, 6-1/8", American, c. 1982, **C.**

1333 Snoopy/Penny, 6-1/8", Korean, c. 1970, **C.**

1334 Snoopy/Savings, 5-3/8", American, c. 1958, **C.**

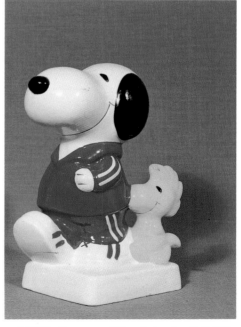

1335 Snoopy/Woodstock, 5-3/8", Korean, c. 1970, **C.**

1336 Robin, 7", American, c. 1965, **C.**

1337 Batman, 7", American, c. 1965, **C.**

1338 Nipper/RCA, 6", American, c. 1970, **B.**

1339 Clicquot Eskimo, 7", American, c. 1950, **D.**

1340 Felix, 6", Japan, c. 1970, **B.**

1341 Miss Piggie, 7-1/2", Japan, c. 1970, **C.**

1342 Santa With Tree, 5-1/2", American, c. 1980, **B.**

1343 Ice Cream Freezer, 4-1/8", American, c. 1980, **B.**

1344 Dordrecht Bank, 7", Holland, c. 1920, **D.**

1345 Bear On Barrel, 5-1/4", Japan, c. 1980, **B.**

1346 Young Black Man, 3-1/2", German, c. 1930, **D.**

1347 Girl With Umbrella, 3-5/8", Japan, c. 1930, **D.**

1348 Humpty Dumpty, 3-1/8", Japan, c. 1935, **C.**

1349 French Peasant, 6-1/2", French, c. 1930, **D.**

1350 Seated Clown, 4-1/2", Japan, c. 1935, **D.**

1351 SBCCA Suitcase Bank, 2-7/8", German, c. 1979, **C.**

1352 Ovoid Bank, 5", France, c. 1875, **D.**

1353 Dollar Bag, 3-1/4", Japan, c. 1950, **B.**

1354 Clown, 5", German, c. 1875, **E.**

1355 Ornate Chest, 2-3/8", France, c. 1880, **E.**

1356 Pagoda Bank, 6", France, c. 1890, **F.**

1357 NYAL Drugstore, 3-1/2", American, c. 1935, **C.**

1358 Fireproof Safe, 1-7/8", American, c. 1930, **E.**

1359 Football Bank, 4-1/4", American, c. 1975, **A.**

1360 Whiskey Jug, 6-1/2", American, c. 1930, **D.**

1361 Mickey and Minnie, 5-1/2", American, c. 1940, **D.**

1362 Wood Canister, 4", France, c. 1870, **E.**

1363 Japanese Bomb,
5-3/4", Japan, c. 1940, **C.**

1364 Statue of Liberty,
7-1/2", Japan, c. 1950, **B.**

1365 Scottie Bank,
5-3/4", American, c. 1940, **B.**

1366 Good Luck Miner, 7", German, c. 1885, **E.**

1367 Register Bank,
8-1/2", Russian, c. 1870, **E.**

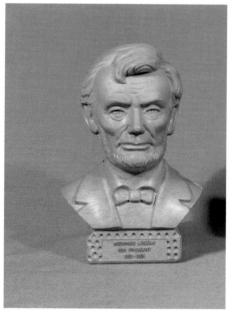

1368 Abraham Lincoln,
5", American, c. 1960, **A.**

CHAPTER 8

MECHANICALS

Some of the most recognizable mechanical banks are presented here from the Steckbeck Collection. It is no surprise that collectors around the world are drawn to the action, beauty and variety of mechanical banks which were initially an American phenomenon. Immediately following the American Civil War, idle foundries were looking for unique toys that would appeal to both children and adults. These charming, colorful, and cleverly designed banks filled the bill. The first known mechanical bank produced from a patent was the *Toy Savings Bank* patented by James Serrill in February, 1869. Ten months later, J. & E. Stevens produced *Hall's Excelsior Bank.* From this modest beginning, the Golden Age of mechanical banks extended for seven decades in America and later in Europe.

The most prolific mechanical bank manufacturer was J. & E. Stevens of Cromwell, Connecticut. With such competent designers as James Hall and Charles Bailey, Stevens led the industry by producing the *Darktown Battery, Girl Skipping Rope* and *Eagle and Eaglets* banks. In 1880, Shepard Hardware Manufacturing Co. of Buffalo, New York, began selling the *Uncle Sam* and *Humpty Dumpty* banks. During this same period, Kyser and Rex of Philadelphia issued the rare *Bowling Alley* and *Lion and Two Monkeys* banks.

Competition and the market success of mechanical banks created an atmosphere for Ives, Judd, Secor and others to enter the field. Finally, Hubley Manufacturing Co. of Lancaster, Pennsylvania, began making the *Trick Dog* and *Organ Grinder* banks. Hubley's

production continued until 1940. Two English companies, John Harper & Co., Ltd. and Chamberlain & Hill, Ltd., furnished mechanical banks for the European market.

Beginning in 1880, Weeden made a series of wind-up tin banks. At the turn of the century, America, England and Germany became leaders in producing a variety of lithographed tin mechanical banks. J. Chein & Co. of New York became the premier manufacturer of tin mechanical banks with their line of clown, elephant, monkey and rabbit banks. Most of the early tin vending banks were made in Germany. Since 1950, John Wright created the Book of Knowledge series of machanical banks using the original patterns. Duro-Mold made a series of space mechanical banks in the 1950s and 1960s. Part of its line was devoted to making a sportsman bank used to advertise Southern Comfort whiskey. Today's mechanical bank market is being satisfied by the production from the Reynolds foundry.

It can be said that mechanical banks reflect the history of their time. By studying each bank, their patents, and catalogs, we are able to piece together a picture of life in a bygone era. Around the world, collectors are preserving these beautiful penny banks for future generations. It is fun to see a child place a coin on William Tell's bow and, by pressing his foot, watch the coin knock the apple off the little boy's head and drop it into the castle. The very next word from the child is, "I want to do that again." We owe Russel Frisbie thanks for designing such a great mechanical bank.

1369 Acrobat Bank, 7-1/4", American, J.& E. Stevens, c. 1883, **C.**

1370 Afghanistan Bank, 3-5/8" w., American, Mechanical Novelty Works, c. 1885, **D.**

1371 American Bank, 5", American, Unknown, c. 1880, **F.**

1372 Artillery Bank, 7-15/16", American, J. & E. Stevens & Shepard Hdwe., c. 1910, **C.**

1373 Atlas Bank, 5-3/4", American, Unknown, c. Ukn., **C.**

1374 Automatic Coin Savings Bank, 5" w., American, Unknown, c. 1890, **D.**

1375 Automatic Savings Bank, 5-7/8"h., German, Saalheimer & Strauss, c. 1930, **F.**

1376 Baby Elephant, 4-1/2", American, C. Bailey, c. 1880, **F.**

1377 Bad Accident, 10-1/4", American, J.& E. Stevens, c. 1891, **C.**

1378 Bank of Education & Economy, 3" w., American, Proctor-Raymond Co., c. 1895, **D.**

1379 Bank Teller Bank, 4-3/8"w., American, J.& E. Stevens, c. 1876, **F.**

1380 Barking Dog, 9-5/8", American, National Company, c. 1910, **D.**

1381 Bear & Tree Stump, 5-3/8"h., American, Judd Mfg. Co., c. 1870, **B.**

1382 Bear, Slot In Chest, 6-7/8"h., American, Kenton, c. 1900, **D.**

1383 Bill E. Grin, 4-1/4"h., American, J.& E. Stevens, c. 1915, **D.**

1384 Billy Goat Bank, 5-1/2", American, J.& E. Stevens, c. 1910, **E.**

1385 Bird On Roof, 4-3/16", American, J.& E. Stevens, c. 1878, **C.**

1386 Bismark Bank, 4-1/8", American, J.& E. Stevens, c. 1883, **E.**

1387 Book-Keeper's Magic Bank, 5"w, American, Unknown, c. Ukn., **B.**

1388 Bow-ery Bank, 4-1/2"w., American, Unknown, c. 1890, **F.**

1389 Bowling Alley Bank, 12-1/4", American, Kyser & Rex, c. 1879, **F.**

1390 Boy And Bull Dog, 4-13/16", American, Judd Mfg. Co., c. 1885, **C.**

1391 Boy On Trapeze, 4-13/16" w., American, J. Barton & Smith Co., c. 1891, **C.**

1392 Boy Robbing Bird's Nest, 6-1/16", J.& E. Stevens, c. 1906, **D.**

1393 Boy Scout Camp, 9-7/8", American, J.& E. Stevens, c. 1915, **D.**

1394 Boys Stealing Watermelon, 6-5/8", American, Kyser & Rex, c. 1894, **C.**

1395 Bread Winners Bank, 10-7/8", American, J.& E. Stevens, c. 1886, **F.**

1396 Bucking Mule, 4-13/16", American, Judd Mfg. Co., c. 1885, **C.**

1397 Bull Dog Bank, 5-5/8", American, J.& E. Stevens, c. 1880, **B.**

1398 Bulldog Savings Bank, 8-3/8", American, Ives, B.& W. Co., c. 1878, **D.**

1399 Bulldog Standing, 3-5/16", American, Judd Mfg. Co., c. 1887, **A.**

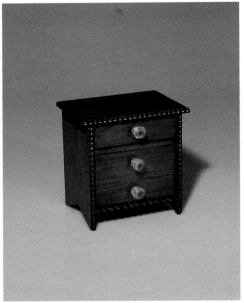

1400 Bureau, J.A. Serrill, 4-7/8"w., American, James A. Serrill, c. 1869, **B.**

1401 Butting Buffalo, 7-11/16", American, Kyser & Rex, c. 1888, **D.**

1402 Butting Goat, 4-3/4", American, Judd Mfg. Co., c. 1885, **C.**

1403 Butting Ram, 6-5/8", American, Wagner & Zwiebel, c. 1895, **F.**

1404 Cabin Bank, 4-3/16", American, J.& E. Stevens, c. 1885, **A.**

1405 Calamity Bank, 7-7/16",
American, J.& E. Stevens, c. 1904,
E.

1406 Called Out Bank, 5-3/4"w.,
American, No Production, c. 1917, **F.**

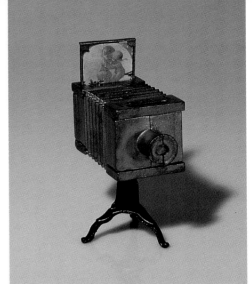

1407 Camera Bank, 4-1/4", American, Wrightsville Hdwe. Co., c. 1890,
D.

1408 Cat & Mouse, Cat Balancing,
5-3/8", American, J.& E. Stevens, c.
1891, **B.**

1409 Chandelers Bank, Ukn.,
American, National Brass Works, c.
1900, **B.**

1410 Chief Big Moon, 10-1/16",
American, J.& E. Stevens, c. 1899,
C.

1411 Chimpanzee Bank, 5-15/16",
American, Kyser & Rex, c. 1880, **C.**

1412 Chinaman In The Boat,
4-3/4", American, C. Bailey, c. 1881,
F.

1413 Chocolat Menier, 4-3/8",
French, L. Revon & Co., c. 1920, **C.**

1414 Circus Bank, 6-3/4"dia., American, Shepard Hdwe. Co., c. 1888, **F.**

1415 Circus Ticket Collector, 3-1/8", American, Judd Mfg. Co., c. 1875, **D.**

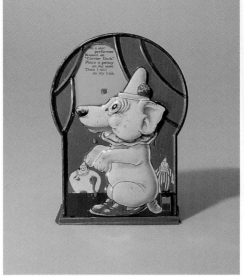

1416 Clever Dick, 5"h., German, Unknown, c. 1920, **B.**

1417 Clown On Bar, 4-3/4", American, C. G. Bush & Co., c. 1880, **F.**

1418 Coin Registering Bank, Ukn., American, Kyser & Rex, c. 1889, **C.**

1419 Columbian Magic Savings Bank, 5-1/8", American, Introduction Co., c. 1892, **A.**

1420 Confectionery Bank, 5-1/4" w., American, Kyser & Rex, c. 1882, **E.**

1421 Cowboy w/ Tray, 6"h., German, Unknown, c. 1920, **D.**

1422 Creedmoor Bank, 9-7/8", American, J.& E. Stevens, c. 1877, **A.**

1423 Crescent Cash Register,
5-7/8"w., American, J. & E. Stevens,
c. 1900, **A.**

1424 Cross Legged Minstrel,
2-5/8" w., England, J. Levey Co., c.
1909, **B.**

1425 Crowing Rooster, 3-1/8"dia.,
German, Keim & Co., c. 1937, **B.**

1426 Cupola Bank, 5-5/8"dia.,
American, J. & E. Stevens, c. 1872,
D.

1427 Dapper Dan, 4-5/8"w., American, Louis Marx & Co., c. 1910, **A.**

1428 Darktown Battery, 9-7/8",
American, J. & E. Stevens, c. 1888,
C.

1429 Darky Fisherman Bank, 6",
American, C. Bailey, c. 1881, **F.**

1430 Darky Watermelon Bank,
11-1/4", American, J. & E. Stevens,
c. 1888, **F.**

1431 Dentist, 9-5/8", American, J. &
E. Stevens, c. 1885, **D.**

1432 Dog On Turntable, 5-7/16",
American, Judd Mfg. Co., c. 1885, **A.**

1433 Dog Tray Bank, 4-5/16",
American, Kyser & Rex, c. 1880, **C.**

1434 Droste Chocolade, 3-3/8"w.,
German, Unknown, c. 1930, **E.**

1435 Eagle & Eaglets, 6-11/16",
American, J.& E. Stevens, c. 1883,
B.

1436 Electric Safe, 3-1/2"w.,
American, Louis Mfg. Co., c. 1904, **A.**

1437 Elephant & Three Clowns, 4-
7/16", American,.& E. Stevens, c.
1883, **C.**

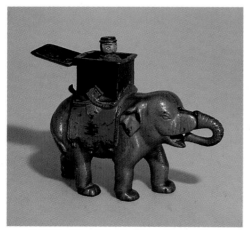

1438 Elephant, Man Pops Out,
4-3/4", American, Enterprise Mfg.
Co., c. 1884, **A.**

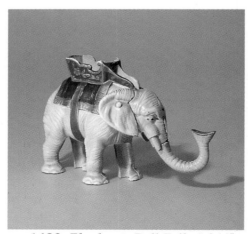

1439 Elephant, Pull Tail, 4-3/4",
American, Hubley Mfg. Co., c. 1930,
A.

1440 Elephant, Swings Trunk,
4-5/8" & 4-7/8", American, A. C. Williams, c. 1905, **A.**

1441 Elephant, Three Stars, 4-5/8", American, Unknown, c. 1884, **A.**

1442 Empire Cinema Bank, Unk., German, Unknown, c. 1913, **F.**

1443 Feed The Goose, 4-1/8", American, Unknown, c. 1927, **A.**

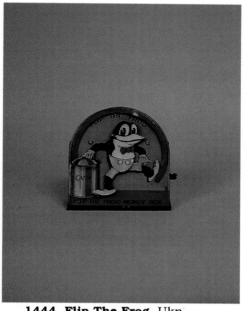

1444 Flip The Frog, Ukn., German, Unknown, c. 1935, **E.**

1445 Football Bank, 10-1/8", English, John Harper & Co., c. 1895, **C.**

1446 Fortune Savings Bank, 3-3/4"h., England, Unknown, c. 1926, **B.**

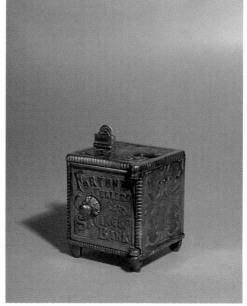

1447 Fortune Teller Savings Bank, 6-3/4"h., American, Baumgarten & Co., c. 1901, **A.**

1448 Fowler, 9", American, J.& E. Stevens, c.1892, **F.**

1449 Freedman's Bank, 6"w., American, Jerome B. Secore, c. 1880, **F.**

1450 Freedman's Bureau,
6-1/8"w., American, Unknown, c. 1880, **C.**

1451 Frog On Arched Track,
7-3/4", American, James Fallows, c. 1871, **F.**

1452 Frog On Rock, 3", American, Kilgore Mfg. Co., c. 1920, **A.**

1453 Frog On Round Base,
4-7/16" dia., American, J.& E. Stevens. c. 1872. **A.**

1454 Fun Producing Savings,
2-3/4", American, Silver-Mirror Co., c. 1918, **C.**

1455 Gem Bank, 5-1/2", American, Judd Mfg. Co., c. 1885, **A.**

1456 Germania Exchange Bank,
4-7/8", American, J.& E. Stevens, c. 1880, **F.**

1457 Giant In Tower, 3-1/2"dia., England, John Harper & Co., c. 1892, **F.**

1458 Giant Standing, 4-3/4", American, Judd Mfg. Co., c. 1870, **F.**

1459 Girl In Victorian Chair, 2-1/8' w., American, W. S. Reed Toy Co., c. 1876, **E.**

1460 Guessing Bank, Man's Figure, 6-1/4"w., American, McLaughlin Brothers, c. 1877, **E.**

1461 Guessing Bank, Woman's Figure, Unknown, American, McLaughlin, c. 1877, **E.**

1462 Gwenda Money Box, 3-5/8", England, Unknown, c. 1930, **C.**

1463 Hall's Lilliput, Tray, 3-3/8", American, J.& E. Stevens, c. 1877, **A.**

1464 Harlequin Bank, 7-3/16", American, J.& E. Stevens, c. 1907, **F.**

1465 Harold Lloyd, 2-3/8", German, Saalheimer & Strauss, c. 1910, **F.**

1466 Hen & Chick, 9-3/4", American, J.& E. Stevens, c. 1901, **C.**

1467 Hindu, 4-1/16", American, Kyser & Rex, c. 1882, **C.**

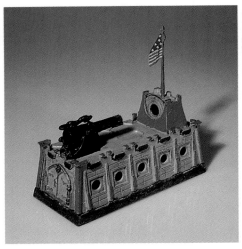

1468 Hold The Fort, 5 Holes, 7-1/4", American, Unknown, c. 1877, **C.**

1469 Home Bank, 3-13/16" w., American, Wm. Morrison, c. 1872, **A.**

1470 Home Bank With Dormers, 4-1/2"w., American, J.& Stevens, c. 1872, **A.**

1471 Horse Race, Straight Base, 4" dia., American, J.& E Stevens, c. 1871, **C.**

1472 Humpty Dumpty Bank, 5" w., American, Shepard Hdwe. Co. c. 1884, **B.**

1473 Huntley & Palmers, Elves, 4-5/8"w., England, Huntley, Bourne & Stevens, c. 1929, **D.**

1474 I Always Did 'Spise A Mule, Boy On Bench, 10-1/8", American, J.& E. Stevens, c. 1897, **B.**

1475 I Always Did 'Spise A Mule, Jockey Over, 10-1/4", American, J.& E. Stevens, c. 1879, **B.**

1476 Ideal Bureau, Ukn., American, Unknown, c. 1905, **A.**

1477 Indian & Bear, 10-3/8",
American, J.& E. Stevens, c. 1883,
C.

1478 Initiating Bank, First Degree,
Uknown, American, Mechanical Novelty Works, c. 1880, **F.**

**1479 Initiating Bank, Second De-
gree,** 7-5/8", American, Mechanical
Novelty Works, c. 1880, **F.**

1480 Japanese Ball Tosser,
3-7/8"w., American, Weeden Mfg. Co.,
c. 1888, **F.**

1481 Jolly Nigger Bank, 4-7/8" w.,
American, J.& E. Stevens, c. 1890,
A.

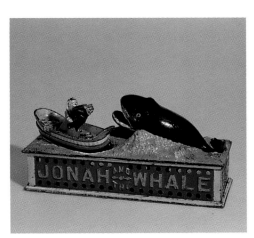

1482 Jonah & The Whale,
10-1/4", American, Shepard Hdwe.
Co., c.1890, **B.**

1483 Jonah, Pedestal, 11-3/16",
American, J.& E. Stevens, c. 1888, **F.**

1484 Kick Inn Bank, 9-1/2", American, Melvisto Novelty Co., c. 1921, **A.**

1485 Leap Frog Bank, 7-1/2",
American, Shepard Hdwe. Co., c.
1890, **C.**

1486 Lehmann London Tower, 1-3/4"w., German, Lehmann, c. 1925, **B.**

1487 Lighthouse Bank, 3-1/8"w American, Unknown, c. 1891, **B.**

1488 Lion & Two Monkeys, 9-1/16", American, Kyser & Rex, c. 1883, **B.**

1489 Lion Hunter, 10-7/8", American, J.& E. Stevens, c. 1911, **C.**

1490 Little Jocko, 5-7/8", American, Strauss Mfg. Corp., c. 1912, **D.**

1491 Lucky Wheel Money Box, 4-1/4"w., England, Jacob & Co., c. 1929, **A.**

1492 Magic Bank, 4-3/4"w., American, J.& E. Stevens, c. 1876, **A.**

1493 Magic Bank, 3-1/4"w., German, Unknown, c. 1935, **F.**

1494 Mama Katzenjammer, 4" w., American, Kenton Mfg. Co., c. 1900, **F.**

1495 Mammy & Child, 4-1/16", American, Kyser & Rex, c. 1884, **C.**

1496 Mason Bank, 7-1/2", American, Shepard Hdwe. Co., c. 1887, **C.**

1497 Memorial Money Box/Liberty Bell, 4-3/4"w., American, Enterprise Mfg. Co., c. 1884, **A.**

1498 Mickey Mouse, Accordion, 3-1/2"w., German, Saalheimer & Strauss, c. 1920, **F.**

1499 Mikado Bank, 5"w., American, Kyser & Rex, c. 1886, **F.**

1500 Milking Cow, 9-7/8", American, J.& E. Stevens, c. 1880, **D.**

1501 Monkey & Coconut, 5-1/8", American, J.& E. Stevens, c. 1886, **C.**

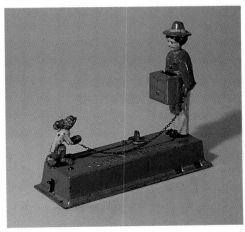

1502 Monkey Bank, 8-13/16", American, Hubley Mfg. Co., c. 1920, **A.**

1503 Monkey, Coin In Stomach, 2-3/4, American, Unknown, c. 1882, **D.**

1504 Monkey, Tips Hat, 2-1/2"dia., American, J. Chein Co. c. 1940, **A.**

1505 Monkey With Tray, 3-1/8"w., German, Maienthau & Wolff, c. 1908, **A.**

1506 Mosque Bank, 6-1/16"w., American, Judd Mfg. Co., c. 1885, **C.**

1507 Mule Entering Barn, 8-1/2", American, J.& E. Stevens, c. 1880, **B.**

1508 Musical Church, 4"w., German, Karl Rohrseitz, c. 1930, **D.**

1509 Musical Savings Bank, 2-3/4"w., German, Unknown, c. 1923, **F.**

1510 National Bank, 5-7/8"w., American, J.& E. Stevens, c. 1873, **E.**

1511 National, Your Savings, 4-3/4", American, Unknown, c. 1900, **A.**

1512 New Bank. 4-1/2", American, J.& E. Stevens, c. 1870, **A.**

1513 North Pole Bank, 3-5/16",
American, J.& E. Stevens, c. 1910, **F.**

1514 Novelty Bank, 4-5/16",
American, J.& E. Stevens, c. 1873,
B.

1515 Octagonal Fort Bank, 11",
American, Unknown, c. 1890, **D.**

1516 Old Woman In The Shoe,
7-5/8", American, W.S. Reed Toy Co.,
c. 1883, **F.**

1517 Organ Bank, Cat & Dog,
5-3/8", American, Kyser & Rex, c.
1882, **A.**

1518 Organ Bank, Medium, 4" w.,
American, Kyser & Rex, c. 1881, **A.**

1519 Organ Bank, Miniature,
3-1/4", American, Kyser & Rex, c.
1890, **B.**

1520 Organ Grinder & Bear,
6-15/16", American, Kyser & Rex, c.
1890, **D.**

1521   Owl, Slot In Book, 2-5/16"
w., American, Kilgore Mfg. Co., c.
1920, **A.**

1522 Owl, Slot In Head, 2-5/16",
American, Kilgore Mfg. Co., c. 1920,
B.

1523 Owl, Turns Head, 3-7/8",
American, J.& E. Stevens, c. 1880,
A.

1524 Paddy And The Pig, 7-1/8",
American, J.& E. Stevens, c. 1882,
C.

1525 Panorama Bank, 4-7/8",
American, J.& E. Stevens, c. 1876,
D.

1526 Patronize The Blind Man,
6-13/16", American, J.& E. Stevens,
c. 1878, **D.**

1527 Peg-Leg Beggar, 3-5/8",
American, Judd Mfg. Co., c. 1880, **D.**

1528 Pelican, Man Thumbs Nose,
5-3/8", American, J.& E. Stevens, c.
1878, **B.**

1529 Perfection Registering,
5-1/4", American, J.& E. Stevens, c.
1893, **F.**

1530 Piano Bank, 5-3/4",
American, E.M. Roche, c. 1900, **F.**

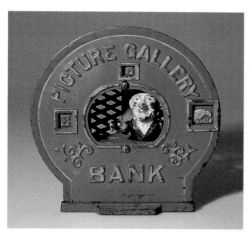

1531 Picture Gallery Bank,
5-3/4"w., American, Shepard Hdwe.
Co., c. 1885, **E.**

1532 Pig In Highchair, 2-3/4",
American, J.& E. Stevens, c. 1897,
B.

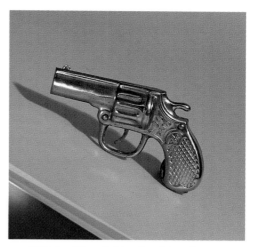

1533   Pistol Bank, 5-3/4", American, Richard Elliot Co., c. 1909, **B.**

1534 Popeye Knockout Bank,
3-1/2"w., American, Straits Mfg. Co.,
c. 1919, **B.**

1535 Preacher In Pulpit, 7-1/8",
American, J.& E. Stevens, c. 1876, **F.**

1536 Presto Bank, 3-7/8" w.,
American, Kyser & Rex, c. 1894, **A.**

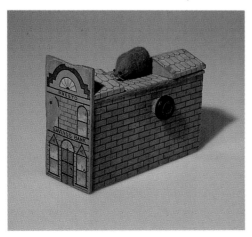

**1537 Presto Savings, Mouse On
Roof,** 6-3/8",   American, Frederick
& Charles, c. 1884, **F.**

**1538 Presto, Penny Changes To
Quarter,** 4-7/8" , American, Henry C.
Hart Mfg. Co., c. 1884, **F.**

1539 Professor Pug Frog, 10-3/16",
American, J.& E. Stevens, c. 1886,
D.

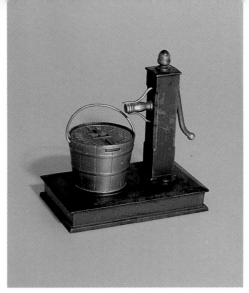

1540 Pump & Bucket, 5-3/4",
American, Unknown, c. 1892, **C.**

1541 Punch & Judy, 6-1/8", American, Shepard Hdwe. Co., c. 1884, **B.**

1542 Punch & Judy, Iron & Tin,
3-3/8"w., England, Stella Works,
c. 1929, **F.**

1543 Rabbit In Cabbage, 4",
American, Kilgore Mfg. Co., c. 1920,
A.

1544 Rabbit Standing, Large,
4-1/4", American, Lockwood Mfg. Co.,
c. 1882, **B.**

545 Rabbit Standing, Small,
2-7/8", American, Lockwood Mfg. Co.,
c. 1882, **B.**

1546 Reclining Chinaman, 8-3/8",
American, J.& E. Stevens, c. 1882,
D.

1547 Red Riding Hood, 4-1/8",
American, W.S. Reed Toy Co., c. 1880,
F.

**1548 Registering Dime Savings
Bank,** 4-1/2"w., American, Ives,
Blakeslee & Williams Co., c. 1890, **A.**

1549 Rival Bank, 4-3/8", American, J.& E. Stevens, c. 1878, **F.**

1550 Robot Bank, 4-3/4"w., England, Starkie's, c. 1910, **F.**

1551 Roller Skating Bank, 8-1/2", American, Kyser & Rex, c. 1880, **F.**

1552 Rooster Bank, 3-1/2", American, Kyser & Rex, c. 1880, **A.**

1553 Royal Trick Elephant, 5-1/2", German, Unknown, c. 1912, **D.**

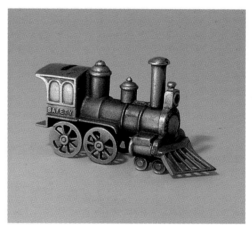

1554 Safety Locomotive, 5-3/4", American, Unknown, c. 1887, **B.**

1555 Saluting Sailor, 4-1/8"w., German, Saalheimer & Strauss, c. 1935, **C.**

1556 Sam Segal's Aim To Save, 12-1/2", American, Samuel Segal, c. 1900, **F.**

1557 Santa Claus Bank, 4-1/8", American, Shepard Hdwe. Co., c. 1889, **B.**

1558 Savo Bank, 2-1/2" high, American, Unknown, c. 1930, **A.**

1559 Schley Bottling Up Cervera, 5", American, Unknown, c. 1898, **F.**

1560 Scotchman, 3-5/8"w., German, Saalheimer & Strauss, c. 1930, **A.**

1561 Seek Him Frisk Bank, 11-3/4", American, Unknown, c. 1881, **F.**

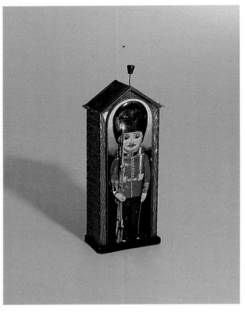

1562 Sentry Bank, 3-1/4"w., German, Unknown, c. 1925, **B.**

1563 Shoot That Hat Bank, 4-3/4", American, Judd Mfg. Co. & Mechanical Novelty Works, c. 1882, **F.**

1564 Shoot The Chute, 9-13/16 American, J.& E. Stevens, c. 1906, **F.**

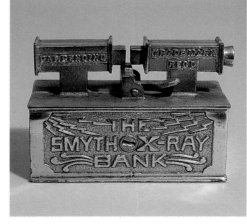

1565 Smyth X-Ray, 5-3/16", American, Henry C. Hart Mfg. Co., c. 1898, **D.**

1566 Snake And Frog In Pond, 5-1/4", German, Unknown, c. 1920, **F.**

1567 Snap-it Bank, 3", American, Judd Mfg. Co., c. 1887, **A.**

1568 Speaking Dog Bank, 7-3/16", American, J.& E. Stevens, c. 1900, **B.**

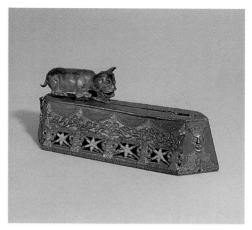

1569 Springing Cat, 9", American, Charles A. Bailey, c. 1882, **F.**

1570 Spring-jawed Alligator, 3-1/2" h., German, Unknown, c. 1930, **F.**

1571 Starkies Aeroplane, 5-1/2", England, Unknown, c. 1930, **F.**

1572 Stollwerk Bros., 3"w., German, Stollwerk Bros., c. 1920, **B.**

1573 Stump Speaker Bank, 5" w., American, Shepard Hdwe. Co., c. 1886, **C.**

1574 Tabby Bank, 2-1/2"dia., American, Unknown, c. 1887, **B.**

1575 Tammany Bank, 4-7/16", American, J.& E. Stevens, c. 1873, **A.**

1576 Tank & Cannon, 7-1/2",
England, Starkie's, c. 1919, **B.**

1577 Target Bank, 7", American,
J.& E. Stevens, c. 1877, **F.**

1578 Teddy & The Bear, 10-1/8
American, J.& E. Stevens, c. 1907,
C.

1579 Thrifty Animal Bank,
3-3/4"w., American, Buddy "L" Co.,
c. 1940. **B.**

1580 Thrifty Scotchman, 8-1/8",
European, Unknown, c. 1935, **E.**

1581 Thrifty Tom's Jigger Bank,
4-5/8"w., American, Ferdinand
Strauss Corp., c. 1910. **A.**

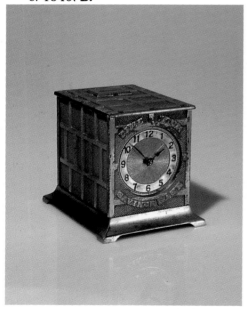

1582 Time Lock Savings Bank,
4-1/8"w., American, Louis Mfg. Co.,
c. 1892, **F.**

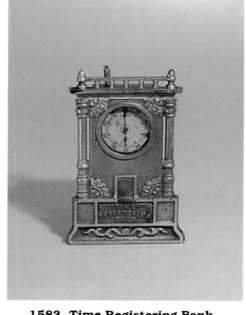

1583 Time Registering Bank,
4-3/4"w., American, Ives, Blakeslee
& Williams Co., c. 1881, **B.**

1584 Tit-Bits Money Box, 2-3/4",
German, Lehmann, c. 1889, **E.**

1585 Toad On Stump, 3-5/8",
American, J.& E. Stevens, c. 1880,
A.

1586 Trick Dog, 6-Part Base,
8-3/4", American, Hubley Mfg. Co.,
c. 1896, **B.**

1587 Trick Dog, Solid Base,
8-3/4", American, Hubley Mfg. Co.,
c. 1920, **A.**

1588 Trick Pony Bank, 7-1/16",
American, Shepard Hdwe. Co.,
c. 1885, **B.**

1589 Turtle Bank, 3-3/4", American, Kilgore Mfg. Co., c. 1920, **F.**

1590 Uncle Remus Bank, 3-3/4",
American, Kyser & Rex, c. 1891, **D.**

1591 Uncle Sam Bust, 3-1/2"w.,
American, Ives, Blakeslee & Williams
Co., c. 1890, **B.**

1592 Uncle Tom, Lapels With Star,
4-1/8" w., American, Kyser & Rex, c.
1882, **A.**

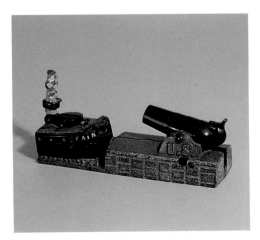

1593 U.S. & Spain, 8-3/8", American, J.& E. Stevens, c. 1898, **C.**

1594 U.S. Bank, Building, 5-7/8",
American, J.& E. Stevens, c. 1872, **E.**

1595 United States Bank,
3-5/8"w., American, Uknown,
c. 1880, **C.**

1596 Watch Bank, 2"dia., American,
Charles L. Russell, c.1920, **C.**

1597 Watchdog Safe, 4-1/2" w.,
American, J.& E. Stevens, c. 1890,
A.

1598 Weeden's Plantation, 3-7/8",
American, Weeden Mfg. Co., c. 1888,
C.

1599 Whale Bank, 5-1/4",
American, Unknown, c. 1930, **A.**

1600 William Tell Bank, 10-9/16",
American, J.& E. Stevens, c. 1896,
B.

1601 Winner Savings Bank, 5",
American, Berger & Medan Mfg., c.
1895, **F.**

1602 Wireless Bank, 6-5/8"w.,
American John Hugo Mfg. Co., c.
1920, **A.**

1603 Wood Face, 2-3/8"dia., European, Unknown, c. 1930, **E.**

1604 Wooden Woman Bank, 3-1/2"dia., European, Unknown, c. 1930, **E.**

1605 Woodpecker Bank, 5-1/4"w., German, Gebruder Bing, c. 1896, **F.**

1606 World's Fair Bank, 8-1/4", American, J.& E. Stevens, c. 1893, **B.**

1607 Zig Zag Bank, 12-1/4" h., American, Kyser & Rex, c. 1889, **F.**

1608 Zoo Bank, 4-1/4" w., American, Kyser & Rex, c. 1894, **B.**

BIBLIOGRAPHY

Barenholtz, Bernard and Inez McClintock. *American Antique Toys, 1830-1900*. New York: Abrams, 1980.

Barenholtz, Edith. *The George Brown Toy Sketchbook*. Princeton: Pyne Press, 1971.

Calvert, Green, Heininger, MacLeod & Vandell. *A Century of Childhood 1820-1920*. Rochester: Strong Museum, 1984.

Davidson, Al. *Penny Lane*. Mokelumne Hill: Long's Americana, 1980.

Duer, Don. *A Penny Saved, Still and Mechanical Banks*. Atglen: Schiffer, 1993.

Duer, Don and Bettie Sommer. *The Architecture of Cast Iron Penny Banks*. Orlando: American Limited Editions, 1983.

Foley, Daniel J. *Toys Through The Ages*. Radnor: Chilton Book Co., 1962.

Fraser, Antonia. *A History of Toys*. London: Hamlyn, 1972. Freeman, Larry and Ruth. *Cavalcade of Toys*. New York: Century House, 1942.

Gould, Mary Earle. *Antique Tin & Toleware*. Rutland: Tuttle, 1957. Guilland, Harold F. *Early American Folk Pottery*. Radnor: Chilton Book Co., 1971.

Hertz, Louis. *Mechanical Toy Banks*. Haber, 1947.

_____. *The Toy Collector*. New York: Funk & Wagnalls, 1969.

Hornung, Clarence P. *Treasury of American Design*, Vol. II. New York: Abrams, 1972.

Kauffman, Henry J. *Early American Ironwork: Cast & Wrought*. Rutland: Tuttle, 1966.

Ketchum, William C., Jr. *Toys and Games*. Washington: Cooper-Hewitt Museum, Smithsonian Institution, 1981.

_____. *American Country Pottery*. New York: Knopf, 1987.

King, Constance Eileen. *The Encyclopedia of Toys*. New York: Crown, 1978.

_____. *Money Boxes*. London: Lutterworth Press, 1983.

Linton, Calvin D., Ph.D. *The Bicentennial Almanac*. Nashville: Nelson, 1975.

Long, Earnest and Ida, and Jane Pitman. *Dictionary of Still Banks*. Mokelumne Hill: Long's Americana, 1980.

Lynd, Robert. *The Money Box*. Appleton, 1926. MacGregor, T. D. *Book of Thrift*. New York: Funk & Wagnalls, 1915.

McClintock, Marshall and Inez. *Toys In America*. Washington: Public Affairs Press, 1961.

McClinton, Katharine Morrison. *Antiques of American Childhood*. New York: Bramhall House, 1970.

Meyer, John D. and Larry Freeman. *Old Penny Banks*. Watkins Glen: Century House, 1960.

Moore, Andy and Susan. *The Penny Bank Book*. Atglen: Schiffer, 1984.

Norman, Bill. *The Bank Book*. San Diego: Accent Studios, 1984.

O'Brien, Richard. *The Story of American Toys*. New York: Abbeville, 1990.

Opie, Iona and Robert, and Brian Anderson. *The Treasures of Childhood*, New York: Arcade, 1989.

Pressland, David. *The Art of the Tin Toy*. New York: Crown, 1976.

Rogers, Carole G.. *Penny Banks, A History And A Handbook*. New York: E. P. Dutton, 1977.

Sanders, Clyde A., and Dudley C. Gould. *History Cast in Metal*. Cast Metals Institute, American Foundrymen's Society, 1976.

Schlesinger, Arthur M., Jr. *The Almanac of American History*. New York: Bramhall House, 1983.

Webster, Donald Blake. *Decorated Stoneware Pottery of North America*. Rutland: Tuttle, 1971.

White, Gwen. *Antique Toys And Their Background*. New York: Arco, 1971.

Whiting, Hubert B. *Old Iron Still Banks*. Manchester: Forward, 1968.

VALUES REFERENCE

The Values Reference is based on the current market values of banks taking into account the number available, condition, color and desirability. The Reference should act pnly as a guide to bank values. Broken, chipped and rusty banks command much lower values. Near mint banks, of course, can set record values. Values are shown in U. S. dollars ($) and with the ratings **A** through **F** as noted in the picture captions for each particular chapter. The use of the Values Reference is subject to the discretion of the seller and the buyer.

Chapter 1. Cast Iron
Pages 10-32

#1-207

A	$75-150
B	100-250
C	175-475
D	350-1,000
E	750-3000
F	Rare

Chapter 2. Ceramics
Pages 34-83

#208-657

Prior to 1930

A	$35-75
B	60-125
C	100-225
D	175-325
E	275-500
F	Rare

1930-1953

A	$25-50
B	35-75
C	50-125
D	100-150
E	125-225

Reduce values by 50% for ceramic banks made after 1953.

Chapter 3. Lead and White Metal
Pages 85-108

#658-873

Prior to 1930

A	$25-65
B	50-110
C	80-150
D	125-525
E	500-1200
F	Rare

1930-present

A	$15-45
B	35-75
C	60-90
D	85-150
E	140-250

Chapter 4. Silver and Brass

Silver and Silver Plated
Pages 110-

#874-

Values may increase if banks are Sterling Silver.

A	$100-150
B	125-225

C	200-350
D	275-550
E	500-2,000
F	Rare

Brass
Pages 126-129

#1018-1053

A	$25-75
B	45-200
C	175-350
D	325-1,000
E	800-2,000

Chapter 5. Tin
Pages 131-143
Pages 154-155

#1054-1170 and 1261-1278

A	$25-65
B	45-90
C	75-150
D	140-300
E	250-550
F	Rare

Dime Registers
Pages 144-146

#1171-1197

A	$50-75

B	65-110
C	100-150
D	140-250
E	240-500
F	Rare

Pocket Banks
Pages 147-153

#1198-1260

A	$20-50
B	45-85
C	80-120
D	100-175
E	170-260
F	Rare

Chapter 6. Wood, Glass and Paper

Wood
 Pages 157-159

#1279-1305

A	$30-50
B	45-75
C	70-125

D	120-150
E	140-200
F	Rare

Glass Banks
Page 160

#1306-1314

A	$10-25
B	20-35
C	30-55
D	50-110
E	100-325
F	Rare

Paper Banks
Page 161

#1315-1323

A	$10-25
B	20-35
C	30-55
D	50-120
E	100-325
F	Rare

Chapter 7. New Finds
Pages 162-167

#1324-1368 Consult the appropriate chapters by material.

Chapter 8. Mechanical Banks
Pages 169-195

#1369-1608

Near Mint condition mechanical banks can command higher values. These values pertain to *cast iron* mechanical banks only. *Wood and tin* mechanical bank values are not included.

A	$500-1,500
B	1,000-2,000
C	2,000-4,500
D	4,000-12,000
E	12,000-30,000
F	Rare

INDEX

About the author

Don Duer is an architect who practices in Winter Park, Florida. He has collected toys and penny banks for over 25 years, dedicating many hours to promoting the hobby of preserving still and mechanical banks of all types.

Don's first book, *The Architecture of Cast Iron Penny Banks* (1983), coincided with a major architectural bank exhibition at the Cooper-Hewitt Museum in New York City. His second book, *A Penny Saved, Still and Mechanical Banks* (1993), presents a complete history of penny banks in America from the 18th century to 1993.

Duer served as president of the Still Bank Collectors Club of America (SBCCA) from 1988 to 1990. He is presently the editor of *Penny Bank Post*, a premier club magazine published by the SBCCA. He has written numerous articles on banks and antiques as a contributing editor for *Inside Collector* magazine.

Recently, Duer was appointed curator of the Winter Park Historical Museum. He and his wife Christine buy, sell and collect penny banks from around the world.